A WELL-BAKED PIE

ARMINLEAR

Library of Congress Control Number: 2022935724

ISBN (paperback): 978-1-956450-21-7
(eBook): 978-1-956450-22-4

 Armin Lear Press Inc
215 W Riverside Drive, #4362
Estes Park, CO 80517

A WELL-BAKED PIE

The 4-Year Practical College Guide
to Launch Your Corporate Career

Brian Ladyman

ARMINLEAR

*This book is dedicated to my beautiful wife, Tracy,
who has been my 30-year travel companion on our
amazing life adventure—and to our terrific children,
Bennet and Greta.
I can't envision a time before you were all in my life.
I'm a lucky man.
Love, b*

GUIDE TO THE GUIDE

ME

Your virtual mentor and friend for the next four years

I love that you have this book in your hand. You are going to read a lot of books over the next four years. Books that will go deep into a wide variety of knowledge areas across core requirements, electives, and your major. All that learning is important in expanding your mind. **But it doesn't help you land a job.**

This book helps you land a job. It is about giving you your best shot at launching well onto a professional career path. I'm here to make your life easier. And, while it may make your life easier if you follow my guidance, that doesn't mean you won't be working hard. There is only value in this book if you take the advice and put it to work.

Mentor = an experienced and trusted advisor

Think of me as your mentor and friend. I will have to earn your trust, but let's talk about my experience.

An enthusiastic passion to help people launch their careers

In the summer of 2017, I decided I wanted to explore being a college professor. I met with the head of the marketing department at the Albers School of Business and Economics, Seattle University. I was just checking out how it worked but, after a short conversation, he said if I was interested, I could teach Strategic Brand Management as an Adjunct Professor that fall. Professor Ladyman. Cool. That was easy. I taught that fall. I taught again in the fall of 2018. And then remotely the spring of 2020 and 2021. All up, I've had just over 100 MBA students through my classes.

Beyond class time, I hold office hours. There, I review résumés. I talk about jobs and career paths. I give career counseling advice. I'm always happy to see that my guidance is a newsflash and super helpful for students. Many are beyond their undergraduate days and still lack understanding of some of the basics for getting on a career track.

I've also been through a few rounds of student mentees—guiding and coaching them on their résumés, networking, interviewing, communicating, and more. I have counseled my son, a 2018 UCLA graduate, and now gainfully employed adult working in the public relations department at T-Mobile. I've counseled my daughter, class of 2022 at WSU as she embarks on her path. I've talked with a lot of other parents on how their kids are doing at school.

In my corporate world, I've also hired and worked closely with hundreds of people along the way. I've seen the attributes and actions of those who get on the fast track, as well as those who struggle getting both hired, and moving ahead.

I know some stuff that works. And I want to share it all.

It's about *you*.

I wrote this book to help scale my advice—to reach more college-aged young adults. You.

Some don't have parents or mentors who have the expertise or time to help write a compelling résumé, encourage setting up LinkedIn at the right time, assist crafting professional emails, develop a strategy to make the most of on-campus career fairs, or negotiate a job offer. Some may have parents who can guide and support on all these things, but not be in the headspace to take their parents advice. Others may have the guidance and innate know-how—taking all the right steps, at all the right times, to land their dream job. Wherever you are, this book can help.

A Well-Baked Pie is intended to create a more level playing field on how the working world works—and how to land a corporate job after graduation. Roughly two million undergraduates enter the working world each year. I promise, there are not two million amazing entry-level jobs out there. Those at the best companies are scarce, and there is a lot of competition for each and every one. Many graduates end up underemployed (working in a job that doesn't require a college degree).

Some think, oh I'll figure it out after I graduate. Not a good plan. Once a couple years pass off the corporate track, it's hard to get on it. Business moves fast, and leaves many behind.

You aren't left behind though. You have this book.

My journey, an unpredictable and energizing ride

You can skip this part if you want to just cut to the meaty action stuff. If you want to know a little bit about my career journey and more on my credibility to be doling out advice, read on. No offense taken if you don't need to know. Whether you read, or skip, there are two important points.

1. Don't stress so much about your first job or first company. You aren't going to retire there. You are going to learn and grow wherever you land. You are going to understand more about what you like to do day to day, what you are good at, not good at, and what type of company culture helps you thrive.

2. You can't plan it all out. I've had an interesting career with many different paths—none of

which I necessarily planned for, or thought much about, in advance of the very next step. It's all good. Your career truly is a journey and one that you can't predict, or see, until it unfolds. Be patient, work hard and smart, network, watch for opportunities, and enjoy the ride.

I graduated with a BS in Business Administration from Pepperdine University in December 1988, moved to Seattle, and job hunted. It was not fun. I ended up accepting a job at Boeing as a Materials Requirements Planning Analyst in a windowless building in Renton, WA. I started on a Monday. I couldn't help but notice that everyone looked "really old" but I realize that was my warped sense of age at the time and they were probably more like thirty or forty instead of fifty or sixty. I was not excited, but I was done job hunting! Yay. I was waiting on another job that I was excited about, but their process was very long, and Boeing was going to take back my offer if I didn't accept. I needed the money.

Learning: Your first job will not be your last and it's okay if you don't love it.

Tuesday afternoon, they called from the company I was excited about and verbally offered me the job. It was more pay. It allowed me to be a part of a cohort of twelve management trainees all my age, give or take a year or two. It was in downtown Seattle. It was part of a program where I would be invested in and trained.

Dilemma: I couldn't quit on Boeing—could I? I spoke to my parents as I struggled with what to do. My dad said it best, "Boeing hasn't invested in you yet, if you're going to quit, now is the time." On Thursday, I had the official paperwork from Bank of America. On Friday, I quit Boeing.

> *Learning: You can't see ahead even a day—I envisioned years there and it was just five days.*

Those five days at Boeing were meant to be on my life journey. Without them, I wouldn't have fully appreciated when I landed at Bank of America. I wouldn't have understood how important company culture is, and having peers who become your friends, and to be somewhere that continued my learning beyond college. I was a trainee, then a personal banker, and then, at twenty-four, I became the youngest branch manager in the state of Washington. I was managing people at an early age, and I learned a lot. It was a fantastic four-year run. There were 170 branch manager positions, and four regional leaders that managed those 170. Getting one of those jobs was going to be a long wait—a wait I was not up for taking. So, I applied to business schools.

> *Learning: Appreciate where you are and learn all you can.*

I ended up going to the Tuck School at Dartmouth. I still didn't know what I wanted to be when I grew up, so I figured a general management MBA program was the way to go. There seemed to be three primary directions coming out of the program:

1. Wall Street

2. Consumer Packaged Goods (CPG) Brand Management

3. Consulting

Wall Street was not my thing. I knew there was a lot of money to be had on that path, but I wasn't feeling it. CPG Brand Management was interesting to me. General Mills was a big recruiter from the program. I didn't have any marketing on my résumé, so I don't think I made it to the cut of students who interviewed on campus. Minneapolis wasn't on the top of my list of places to live so, looking back, I think that worked out just fine.

Learning: It's okay to be unsure of your career direction—even at thirty.

Then there was consulting. During the summer between my first and second years, I ended up getting a summer internship at A.T. Kearney in New York City. I had a great experience with a massive learning curve and ended up accepting a position in their San Francisco office upon graduation in the spring of 1995. I had some hefty student loans, but in two short years I had lived through an amazing life experience, more than doubled what I made, and put myself onto a new career path. I worked at A.T. Kearney for about two and a half years—including projects in New York City, San Antonio, San Francisco, Chicago, and Sydney. Those years involved some grueling work weeks and a ton of airplanes, but I wouldn't trade them. That said, I didn't see consulting as the career ladder I wanted to climb. The higher you went, the more you traveled. My son was born in 1996 and, after that, leaving on a Sunday red-eye or crack-of-dawn Monday flight was no longer my thing.

Learning: All jobs have trade-offs—I loved the variety of work but burned out on the travel.

I'm going to speed up a bit and condense a decade. When getting my MBA, marketing had always been the functional area that I found most interesting. Through a business school friend, I ended up joining a marketing team at Oracle in late 1997. A couple years later, I leveraged that to get a Director of Corporate Marketing role at a software company in Seattle. This was all during the time of the dotcom bubble and subsequent bubble burst.

Another software company in Charlotte, NC actively recruited me for about six months to come join them to be VP of Marketing and part of their executive team. I eventually made the move and was very glad I did—the path it opened was amazing. The name of the company was YOUcentric. About nine months after joining, they were acquired by J.D. Edwards. J.D. Edwards offered me the VP of Demand Generation Marketing role in Denver. About two years after that, PeopleSoft bought J.D. Edwards. PeopleSoft offered me the role of VP Marketing for Japan and Asia Pacific based in Sydney. It was an incredible gig and I had members of my team in Tokyo, Singapore, Hong Kong, Beijing, and, of course, Sydney. Loved it. Then Oracle bought PeopleSoft and I took a nice monetary package and left. It was a super fun run with a ton of career and life learning.

Learning: Finding your groove feels good and presents lots of opportunities.

The CEO of YOUcentric then recruited me to come work for him again at another software company. This time in Chicago where we landed in February 2005. February is summer in Sydney—warm and toasty summer. February in Chicago means an obsession with the wind-chill factor. From the start, my wife and I wanted to leave. We lived in a neighborhood called Winnetka, where the *Home Alone* house is located. It was beautiful to look at but didn't feel quite right to us. Also, turns out the company technology wasn't ready for prime time. So, about eighteen months in, I started to look for roles back on the West Coast.

Learning: Even when in your groove, not every role or company works out—roll with it.

I liked, and was good at, marketing at tech companies. I thought it was my thing. Well, it turns out it was not my fate to continue leading marketing for a company. I would instead go deeper in digital and come at the marketing work from a services organization perspective. There was still some of the aftermath of the dotcom bubble burst and senior tech company positions were not as prevalent. Through my network, I ended up getting a VP of Strategy position at a digital agency, MRM (McCann Relationship Management) working on the Microsoft account. I could live in San Francisco, or Seattle, but my pay was going to be the same. Given the cost-of-living difference, Seattle was the easy choice. I progressed through numerous senior roles and learned new skills. Eventually though, McCann lost the Microsoft relationship, and the Seattle office was closed.

I quickly jumped ship to another digital agency that focused on Microsoft. It was not a well-run place, but they had a well-paying position open and, at that point, the world was still in the aftermath of the 2007-2009 financial crisis. For a while, I was just happy to have a job in that rough market. However, I needed to find something where I was happy and enthusiastic about showing up every day. I looked around but couldn't find anything that got me excited. By then in my career, I didn't want to work at a behemoth like Microsoft or T-Mobile, and I was kind of past the financial insecurity of working at a start-up. It was the least favorite time of my career, and I could not find a clear path forward. Then, the path found me. Things happen when they are supposed to happen.

Learning: Even when you seem to be off your path, there is still much to learn.

In the summer of 2013, I received an unsolicited LinkedIn message from a recruiter at Slalom Consulting. She was interested in my background. They were looking for somebody to be the Practice Director for their Customer Engagement team in Seattle—somebody who knew consulting, had worked in marketing, and understood digital. Sounded exactly like me. I had never heard of Slalom, but I met her for coffee to see what she had to say. Turns out Slalom is consulting without the airplanes—they focus on building relationships and serving clients within each of their local markets. I think I was on the ground working within three weeks of that first coffee. I have absolutely loved working at Slalom. I've worked with, and led, many different teams over the years and I am currently a Managing Director leading our business consulting team in Seattle.

Learning: Time "off path" may be leading exactly where you are meant to be.

One of the things I love about Slalom is we are encouraged to follow our passion and love our work and life. I was curious about teaching, explored it, and now make time one quarter a year to teach a ten-week evening MBA course. While consulting is my main job, teaching feeds another part of me.

Learning: Keep finding new experiences to feed your growth; teaching was never in my plan.

Toward the end of the year at Slalom, we get holiday cards with vellum (thin paper) with messages from others. They typically have holiday greetings and some sort of shout out of appreciation. Writing them in late November isn't the most fun you can have. I typically write around one hundred of them and it takes a healthy amount of time. It is really nice to receive them though. When I read mine on December 23, 2019, one stood out. It was from my friend Andrew Houston. He suggested my talents were somewhat under-utilized and that, "I feel you should have written your best-selling book by now, and I even have the title for you *STFU and GSD*." That translates to Shut The F*ck Up and Get Sh*t Done. I'm known for being able to get shit done. I pondered his message. Very interesting. I like new things.

On December 27, through the magic of how our sleeping brains work, I woke up at 5:40 a.m. with the idea for this book, and by 5:50 a.m. I was writing. By December 31, I had my full initial outline, 7,500 words, four title and cover options, and the list of amazing people that I knew could give me feedback to improve the content—which they did. And, most importantly, I had a goal to complete it in 2020. Thank you, Andrew, for that nudge of inspiration.

Learning: You never know when inspiration or opportunity will present itself, so stay open.

I'll close this section with the two points where I started. Work hard as you progress through *A Well-Baked Pie*, but don't sweat it if you don't land that first dream job. I have traveled many different roads along the way—all of which taught me new life lessons, skills, and more about what I like and don't like. Also, opportunities present themselves in unexpected ways. Looking back, I could never have predicted that the twists and turns in my career would have resulted in such an interesting journey. Be open to your path. Make the most out of every step along the way—cliché, but legit.

Learning: Even when you think you know where you are headed, you have absolutely no idea. And that's okay.

YOUR JOURNEY

Let's talk about pie (aka you) for a moment

To launch out of college on a career trajectory, you need to stand out. Bear with me as I introduce an analogy that we'll use throughout the book. You are like a pie. Some pie is delicious and totally worth the calories, and some pie, not so much. My job is to help you be the absolute best pie that you can be. That's what recruiters are looking to get—a well-baked pie.

you are the pie!

The seven essential ingredients for a well-baked pie

Before we talk about the seven essential ingredients, let's talk about how hiring works. People hire students who are vibrant. Students who are grounded and comfortable in their skin. Ones who have some spark and can hold a conversation. Ones who are prepared— and passionate. People hire students with some professional polish. If you take the actions in this book, and grow in the seven areas, you will become one of these students that people hire.

Let's get back to you as a pie. A tasty pie all starts with the right mix of ingredients. Typically, the four foundational ingredients of a whole human are heart, body, mind, and spirit. Let's read those again slowly: heart, body, mind, and spirit.

As I think about college life, and getting you prepared for landing a corporate job, those four ingredients alone don't quite give us the framework we need. I've tweaked those four a little and added three more. I may touch on all seven here and there, but my focus will be on the three that are most overlooked in context of landing a professional job post college.

So, here are the seven.

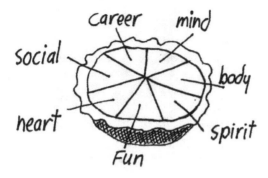

So, what do I mean by each of those seven? Let's start with the four that will not be our focus but are still important.

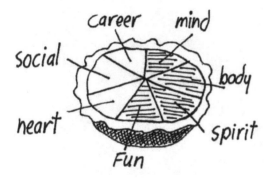

Mind (aka classroom and academic learning)

There are other aspects of the mind beyond academic learning, but for the most part, college is about filling your mind with all kinds of new information, on all kinds of topics. That learning requires you to show up to class, study, work on projects, have anxiety about taking tests, take tests, have relief when completing tests, get good grades, and maybe get some not so good grades. That is all a key part of your college experience. I'm going to assume you have this part covered. If not, there are a ton of books you can read on this topic—and hopefully plenty of support at your school. If you feel like you need help in this area, I strongly encourage you to reach out and get it.

Body (aka health and wellness)

I am a huge fan of exercise and eating healthy. I also love Netflix, our couch, and pizza. In college, there is notably way more pizza than in my world—and the twenty-something metabolism to go with it. The key is balance. There are so many life-long benefits of being healthy. For the purview of landing a job, the vibrancy that comes through from living a healthy and active lifestyle does show up when networking and interviewing. I encourage you to find time to do something that keeps you active during your college years—create some habits around it. Exercise and activity are also a great way to reduce some of your college stress.

Spirit (aka your inner compass)

Spirit is an important aspect of being human. I don't consider myself religious. I can't recall the last time I was in a church—most likely a wedding. However, I am somewhat spiritual and introspective about what it means to be human. I believe there is some kind of higher power but I'm not here to make any commentary on religion. You do you. What I will say is that your college years are a time to explore your beliefs and values. It's a time to fine tune your inner compass and figure out how you think about yourself in the world. Take time for some introspection. On that point, I've been exploring meditation the last couple years. I haven't quite created a habit around it yet, but I am a huge fan of the Headspace app in helping grow in this area. Check it out.

Fun (aka enjoyment as you define it)

Fun, goofing off, chilling—whatever you call it—is important. Really, it *is* important. Make time for fun! How does fun relate to starting a successful career? Fun allows you to show up refreshed for your studies. Fun allows you to reduce your stress levels. Fun typically involves other people, and it grows your social skills. What you do for fun probably makes you more interesting. Make time for fun. There, I said it twice. I have no advice for how you have fun. Just make time for fun. Enough said.

Now let's turn to the three that we'll work on together.

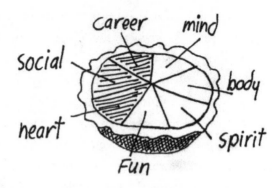

Heart (aka finding and feeding your passion)

The heart is key. What gives you passion? What excites and motivates you? What fulfills you? What job will get you excited to jump out of bed? Yes, I said jump out of bed, not drag your tired ass out of bed. I truly love my job and get excited about going every day. I love my work so much that sometimes I get to my desk by 6 a.m. because I'm so eager to get rolling—not kidding. There are so many people in the world who show up just to get a paycheck—millions. They trudge through their workweeks and live only for days off. You don't have to be one of those people.

There is an extremely high chance you have absolutely no idea what excites and motivates you as it relates to work. That's normal. You want that perception to evolve and change over your four years, which is why I have a ton of advice in this area. Different majors typically lead to a different set of first jobs. If you land a job that feeds your soul in some way, it makes showing up every morning a heck of a lot easier.

In the Heart sections of *A Well-Baked Pie*, our primary focus will be helping you narrow in on the major that feels most on target for who you are, and your interests. We'll also explore your brand and what makes you special as a future job candidate.

Social (aka all aspects of interacting with others)

This one is huge! Huge. First, this is about making friends, becoming comfortable interacting with new people, and building relationships. Social engagement is also an area where some college students don't grow enough during college to successfully interview for corporate positions. I've come across seniors who can barely hold a conversation. Not kidding.

The working world requires a lot of social skills— communicating, collaborating, connecting, interacting, presenting, listening, selling, negotiating, and the list goes on. Employers are looking for your ability to relate to others and use these skills. I have two more important "ing" things to add—network*ing* for a job and interview*ing* for a job. Spending time on this social engagement piece of the pie as it is just as important, if not more, as the mind and academic learning aspects of college. Some of my advice will feel awkward but trust me.

The Social section content all shares one thing in common—it involves you interacting with others and evolving your skills from a senior in high school to a young professional. The skills range from basics like having a strong handshake and good eye-contact to excelling in more specific social interactions like career fairs, networking coffees, video calls, and ultimately, interviewing.

Career (aka tactical actions to put your best foot forward)

If you don't whip up your résumé for the first time until your senior year, chances are you will not find yourself in the greatest position (this is an understatement). You will have missed out on taking actions in your earlier college years that could have set you up to be attractive to employers. I know time management is super hard at college. There is a ton of stress about studying. Everyone wanders around in a state of constant sleep deprivation. And I know graduation can seem a life time away. But, it will be here before you know it.

The Career sections provide tactical tips that will leave you well positioned to interview for internships and full-time roles. Some are quick and easy; some take a bit longer. Topics include detailed advice on getting the attire you'll need to show up confident, creating a stand-out résumé, leveraging LinkedIn, attacking your job search, and negotiating your offer. Please, please, please, find time each year to take the recommended actions. You'll be happy that you did. Again, trust me.

> **Okay pie: the result of not getting your ingredient mix quite right**

Okay pie is just that. It is one in which the mix of ingredients is a little off. Not quite right. Maybe it's missing a little sugar or has more salt than it should. Those mismeasurements make for okay pie. Chances are, without being intentional, you will graduate college being an okay pie—nothing terribly wrong with that. We've all had okay things before. And they're not bad—they're just not the best possible. Great companies are not looking for okay, though. When you are trying to land a highly sought-after job, you need to be a memorable, or even an incredible pie—a buttery, flakey, delicious sensation with the right balance of ingredients across the seven dimensions.

Shitty pie: two college extremes to avoid

Without being intentional, there is a high likelihood you will become an okay pie. There is also a chance though that you could become a shitty pie. Let's talk about two common extremes. You've probably seen the younger version of these in high school. One is obviously not great for landing a corporate job. The second one though seems like it could be great—and it actually takes a lot of hard work and sacrifice. Some students spend their college experience becoming the second type of pie. And that's sad. I don't recommend either of the following.

Shitty pie #1: fun pie

This pie is fun. The name really says it all. Fun pie drinks, parties, and skips class. Fun pie sleeps in and has shitty grades. Fun pie asks to "borrow" other people's notes before a final and then, if having a good day, ekes out a C-. They go out on Tipsy Tuesday, White Claw Wednesday, Thirsty Thursday, and of course Friday and Saturday. While it can be said that fun pie has a total blast in college, fun pie is not prepared to land a top job.

I've met numerous fun pies and most, if not all, wish for a do over. If you identify with this, I strongly encourage you to tone down the partying and carve out time to study and make school a priority. If you haven't left for college yet and are shocked and disappointed to hear that fun pie isn't a good life path, you may want to backburner college. Seriously, save your and/or your parent's money. Stay in your current bedroom at home, or perhaps move to the basement for that extra bit of privacy. Maybe go on a vacation. This approach will still be fun, it will be much cheaper, and your parents don't have to get used to you moving away and then moving back—because you never leave. You'll just be there like you always have been.

If your future self, wanting to get into graduate school, could speak to you, they would also tell you not to be fun pie because your grades can matter after college.

If you're this kind of student and you want to have some fun that might actually make a difference in your career, take a gap year. Spend a year teaching skiing or SCUBA diving if that's your favorite pastime, or volunteer/get an internship in a foreign country where you have to speak a different language and eat strange foods every day. These kinds of "fun" actually can look good on a résumé, and, in the meantime, you might stir some passion for a career path without living in your parents' basement.

Shitty pie #2: mind pie (aka academic learning)

In contrast to fun pie, mind pie has fantastic grades. I mean fantastic. They go to class. They study. They study more. They sleep. They study. They sleep. That's it. Mind pie is also not prepared to land a top job. Academic smarts are not the only thing employers care about—they want the balance of ingredients. Honestly, if you're a straight A student, you might think you are better prepared for the corporate world than fun pie. You might even feel superior to fun pie. I would argue that mind pie will also find it somewhat challenging to land an amazing job.

Balance is key: ebb and flow and, while you're at it, yin and yang

Life is about balance, and college life is really about balance. Think about the seven dimensions and your balance across them. Your focus will ebb and flow. You'll need a little yin and a little yang. Go with it. I leave it with you to keep an ongoing focus on Mind, Body, Spirit, and Fun. There are plenty of ways to get support for your academic learning. I don't think you need a lot of advice on how to start playing sports or exercising—although I will suggest finding a friend who also is into staying fit. Regarding spirit: question. Question and learn throughout your life, not just college. Finally, fun. Have some.

Let's put our focus on Heart, Social, and Career.

Pie doesn't make itself; quoting Nike, just do it

Making a pie requires a lot of action—adding, pinching, separating, sprinkling, blending, mixing, coating, rolling, placing, combining, covering, baking, cooling, and serving. Becoming who you are meant to be is also going to require a lot of action. Lucky for you, I've laid those actions out year by year, step by step—and no one thing is hard or time-consuming. You just need to follow along and do it. If you happen to come from a Running Start or similar program, you'll need to read through a little faster to get to the content related to your actual class standing as a sophomore or junior.

Feel free to skim if you think you have already nailed a particular piece of guidance. The advice in this book applies whether you are an A, B, or C student—honestly, probably not as much if you are a D or F student. It also applies broadly to any business or professional type career direction—for example, accounting, analytics, change management, finance, general management, human resources, information management, management consulting, marketing, operations, sales, user experience, and many others. I come at it from a business career perspective because that is the world I know best. I have to think, though, that much of the guidance applies regardless of your career path.

The important thing is to take action. You'll find "get shit done" sections throughout the book summarizing key actions. Make sure to take those actions. This book is about making steady progress and building new muscles throughout your college experience. New muscles are not created merely by reading about exercise. Also, there is a handy recap at the end of each term to keep track of what you have accomplished. Keep a notepad with you as you go through this book and jot down action items and ideas.

Let's move on to your first term as a freshman! Because everything in your life is so new your first term, I've included a little bit of college context and a couple recommendations. Read about those, take action, and then put the book away until right before you come back from your holiday break. Do crack it open though before you get back into the thick of your second term classes.

Let's go.

FRESHMAN FIRST-TERM

Mainly get settled and fire up your curiosity

First, congratulations on getting to college. Nice work. I say that no matter where you landed. It will be an amazing life experience. For the purposes of this book, I'm going to assume you are living away from home for the first time. If you aren't, then good on you for saving money; some points may not resonate as much, but you'll get the idea.

You can now:

» Stay up all night playing Mario Kart
» Sleep all day
» Skip showering
» Skip brushing and flossing
» Skip class

» Forget about homework
» Wing tests
» Live off Red Bull and coffee
» Binge drink
» Puke (special bonus of binge drinking)
» Smoke or try drugs
» And all around live a hedonistic life of leisure

Amazing right? No, not really. I list these things just to acknowledge some of the realities and temptations that exist—especially for freshman away from their parents for perhaps the first time. You will undoubtedly check off some things on the above list. Maybe you are continuing your partying ways from high school, maybe you are exposed to these things for the first time, or maybe you aren't personally tempted by much from this list. Some of these things are a part of the process of becoming an adult—but make good choices. Be safe. Again, the key is balance. By balance, I really mean the above things should be far eclipsed by the things on this list:

» Studying and going to class
» Being curious about majors and the typical jobs that align to majors
» Trying new activities and getting leadership positions
» Meeting new people and growing your network
» Morphing from a young adult to a young professional

» Being active and exercising

» Getting work experience—for life skills and your résumé

College is different from high school. In high school you are pretty much told what classes to take, and those lead to college. Just do what you are told, and the next phase of life will happen. College, in sharp contrast, can lead to so many different paths. It doesn't just happen. You need to play an active part in your life now—a part you may not be equipped to play well immediately. Whether you are equipped or not, it is your life, and your responsibility. Use the time in college wisely to figure out what the right starting career path is for you—based on your interests, talents, and ambitions.

Now, let me step off my lectern and be real. You are likely living away for the first time. You're learning how to live with a roommate and make new friends. You're finding classes and your rhythm for studying. You're calling and facetiming your parents (do call and facetime them sometimes—they miss you and honestly texting and Snapchat doesn't cut it). You're getting settled into a whole new life. Do all that. Focus on getting settled. This is a big life transition. For that reason, we're going to start slow. I only have two recommendations for your first term—one for heart and one for social.

Heart: Finding your passion

This first topic should be top of mind for your first couple of years. It is an area where many struggle—picking your major. An estimated 75 percent of students switch their major at least once—you can see it is very normal not to finish college on the same path you started. The problem is, if you explore and struggle too long, it adds cost and time. My goal is to help you pick something you are comfortable with sooner.

Before we dig in, let's level set on something. Just because you enjoy a subject, doesn't mean it has to be your major. I enjoy psychology, it's interesting. I never wanted to be a psychologist though. Or perhaps you are passionate about climate change. That doesn't mean you have to be an Environmental Science major. You can take electives and join clubs to feed areas of interest. In contrast, your major should connect to jobs you think will feed your passion on a daily basis, as well as provide a financially viable path for the standard of living you hope to achieve.

Be obsessively curious about majors—and, more importantly, the related jobs

This first thing involves both a mindset and behavior. Be obsessively curious about majors. Let me say it again, be obsessively curious about majors. You want to know things like:

» What do you learn about?
» What is a typical first job out of college? How much does it pay?

» What activities does somebody in that job actually do for 8 to 10 hours every day?

» Do those activities seem like they align to your skills and interests?

» What are some typical jobs ten years down the road? How much do they pay then?

» What are good companies for that type of job?

» Are the jobs available in any city, or are there certain locations better than others?

This curiosity around majors is also a very straightforward way to start conversations with new people and expand your social circle. Everyone there is probably eager to have this conversation to learn. Be the catalyst of curiosity. In addition to chatting people up, visit your college website and find the page that lists all majors. Scroll through and challenge yourself to check out some that you weren't initially considering. Use online search engines to get an understanding of the opportunities that align to different majors. Keep digging deeper with curiosity.

It's likely you will change majors, or at least consider changing major. Many students do. Arming yourself with the most information though will get you closer to the mark, faster, for what might be the right fit for you.

Be curious

What does it look like to be obsessively curious about majors? **It is very simple, ask everyone you meet a few of these:**

- » What's your major?
- » Why did you pick that?
- » What do you like about it? Dislike?
- » What job do you think you might do after you graduate? (You may get some blank stares to this one.)
- » What does a day in the life of that job look like?

...and just take the conversation wherever it goes

Push yourself to meet juniors and seniors to have this conversation—you can benefit from their learning curve and those relationships may help you when you are a senior and they are in the workforce.

Social: Hanging with others

It is important for you to be intentional in growing your social skills. Social skills from high school, are much different than those in the professional world. We'll evolve your skills step-by-step each year. This first term, your social action is very straightforward.

> Get involved—you meet new people and it adds things of interest to your résumé

Getting involved is important for many reasons. Depending on what you get involved in, you're likely to be hitting many or all of the ingredients of a well-baked pie. Getting involved can:

Expand your **mind**—one of the key reasons for being at college

Get your **body** active—through exercise, sports, and activity clubs

Feed your **spirit**—through exploration of what gives you energy

Be **fun**!—it should absolutely be fun

Expand your **social** circle—and the friends you make now will become your network later

Light up your **heart**—helping you discover what gives you passion and what doesn't

Provide fodder for your **career** efforts—providing great content to make you more interesting

Don't be scared to put yourself out there. You are paying money to be at college to grow as a person. At no other time in your life will there be such a variety of things to get involved in with such a light lift to make it happen. Join things—academic clubs, professional clubs, social clubs, theatre, music, sports teams, and so on. It can be something you have always been interested or involved in, or something you know nothing about and want to learn. Be curious. Invest in yourself.

During the first few weeks of school many clubs and groups spend time in the main area of campus talking about what they do while trying to recruit new members. Take the time to stop and learn. Here are some starter questions to fire up conversation:

» What do you do?
» Why do you like being involved?
» How often do you get together?
» What do you typically do when you get together?
» Are there potential leadership opportunities as an upperclassman if you stay involved?

Beyond the open house experience for learning about all the clubs and teams, talk to others, and keep your eyes and ears open for things that sound interesting.

Sororities and fraternities are a fantastic way to grow a tight network of friends. Both of my kids have been involved with Greek life and it's been a solid growth experience for them. Not every campus has a Greek system, and the experience isn't for everyone. One of the career-related benefits of Greek life is that you build relationships with upperclassmen who can be great mentors, are entering the job market ahead of you, and will have learned lessons in a way you'll be able to relate. You can even ask them for résumé review and mock interview practice when the time comes. If you do get involved in Greek life, tap into your network both before and after you graduate.

Jump in

Commit to one or two things to try out—start by exploring three to four potential opportunities before committing. Don't over commit your freshman year. Remember you are focused on getting settled and you can always join more things later.

Freshman first-term recap

I've included recaps so you have easy references of all the topics covered in a term or year. Don't feel bad if you don't always accomplish them all. Your first term is a busy time with lots of life adjusting so we're starting slow with just two things—oh, and two bonus ones. How did it go on these?

Heart: Finding your passion

> » Created a habit of being curious—What's your major? Why did you choose that?

Social: Hanging with others

> » Got involved in at least one to two activities that I am excited about.

You get bonus points (lots of them) if you achieve these life-altering actions. These are no joke.

> » Created a habit of putting my phone in airplane mode while studying and in class.
> » Figured out a planner system to stay on top of everything (for example, Microsoft OneNote or To Do)

Please set a reminder to dig back into *A Well-Baked Pie* a week or so into your holiday break.

FRESHMAN SECOND-TERM

Party still?
Sure, but start the adulting process

You made it through first term! That's huge. Hopefully you are feeling a bit settled in your new life. In your groove for going to classes? Balancing partying and fun with studying? If not, know that for some it takes longer. If you did answer no, I encourage you to start adulting a bit more aggressively. Whether yes or no, I'm going to assume you can put a few more actions on your plate for this second term.

Heart: Defining your passion

I just have one thing in the heart category, and it is very straightforward, although it perhaps may take some work to become second nature.

Double down on curiosity—"tell me more."

Get extra curious. Keep working on learning about different majors and the associated career paths. Take it a step further. Be curious about everything—your classes, your friends, your professors, your emotions.

This curiosity is critical for two reasons. The first: The more you learn about yourself during college, the more confidence you will have when interviewing for jobs. There is also a higher probability that you'll be interviewing for jobs that align to your interests.

The second reason: Being curious with others is a great way to build relationships. People like people who are interested in what they have to say. I work with somebody who says, "be interested, to be interesting." So true. By the way, Dale Carnegie said it originally. Anyway, be curious to learn from, and about, others. You'll learn, and you'll also strengthen relationships. I have two phrases to get into your conversation repertoire:

"Tell me more."

"What else?"

What does it look like? Pretend a friend has just finished a thought about growing up in Alaska. Say, "tell me more." When they tell you more, listen. Then try some variation of, "What else?" to dig deeper into their story. What else was different growing up in Alaska? What else did you love about living there? What else? Tell me more. Rinse and repeat with any topic.

Try these two phrases and related variations with your friends. Then lean forward and listen. Both are fantastic for diving deeper into a conversation. This curiosity will serve you well when you are in conversations with employers as they love a curious, learner mindset.

Go deeper

Add these to your conversation repertoire:

"Tell me more."

"What else?"

Social: Developing soft skills

For this second term, I've got a few actions all geared around growing your soft skills as they relate to social interaction. The first one is quick and easy—learn about your semester abroad program. The second will require work for some and be second nature to others. The final one will likely be something nobody is a fan of doing. All I ask is that you try it out.

Learn about semester abroad—an easy thing to make you more interesting

Living abroad is a fantastic way to mature your social skills. You meet new people. You learn new cultural norms. Your mind expands with new ideas and experiences that push you beyond your comfort zone. Living abroad enriches your college experience and shows that you are someone who can go out of their comfort zone and adapt to new environments. It makes you a more interesting person in real life—and a more interesting person on your résumé. Plus, it is an amazing life experience and off the charts on the fun scale.

Not all colleges offer a semester abroad. If your school does, take an hour to learn about what they offer. The tuition cost for a semester abroad is typically the same as the main campus, however there are of course additional travel costs. Find out how the program works at your school. Understand if it will be financially viable for you and look into scholarships or grants that you can use. If you can afford it, start to think about where you want to go and understand the classes that are offered there. You'll want to share your intentions with your academic advisor as you plan out your sophomore year classes.

Schools advise differently on the best time to go abroad. I spent the summer semester between my sophomore and junior years in London, right in the center of Knightsbridge. I used to grab lunch in the Harrod's food halls. Those few months were an absolute highlight of my college experience. I had an amazing time—living in London and traveling to France, Germany, Austria and Spain. It also made me a more interesting person to potential employers. Living abroad seems to accelerate maturity and infuse a new level of confidence.

See the world

Go to the office for your study abroad program, read a brochure, talk to somebody about your interest, and figure out if it is viable for you.

Equip with a few body language basics—it will take you far

This is probably more relevant in the later college years when interviewing becomes more prevalent. It's here in the freshman year section to get the concept across early since these three things are great for basic social interaction with others at school too.

Today there is a mix of greeting types—fist bump, elbow bump, handshake, perfunctory hug, big close bear hug, and, much more commonly, the awkwardness of not knowing which one the other person will use. Handshakes honestly need the most focus to get right. I cannot tell you how many young adults I have interacted with across the years that have terrible handshakes—sweaty, limp, just fingers! A bad handshake is an instant turn-off when I am meeting candidates. For me, a weak or weird handshake communicates a lack of confidence. I'm not looking for that in candidates. I, like many employers, am looking for someone who conveys confidence and warmth.

Simply extend your hand, make eye contact, and shake the person's hand—somewhere between a bone-crushing grip and flaccid interaction. If you think your palm is sweaty, maybe due to nervousness, subtly dry it before shaking the person's hand.

Poor eye contact is not as instantly noticeable as a poor handshake, but it is noticeable. Good eye contact shows the person talking to you that you're listening—it makes them feel heard (even if you are daydreaming while they're talking, which hopefully you aren't). It shows interest, intensity, presence, focus, and connection. Good eye contact can unconsciously support connection between people, which helps people remember each other and relate. Keep in mind, though, that this is body language relating to Western culture; Eastern cultures do not necessarily value or appreciate direct eye contact in the same way. Be mindful of who are you interacting with.

Eye contact comes very natural to some, and not as much to others. If you're not sure if you have good eye contact, ask your friends.

Finally, speak clearly; don't mumble. Don't make the person you are speaking with have to express that they can't hear you. If this is a challenge for you, please keep working at it. You are at college to learn and grow so don't feel bad about your starting point, just work to improve. Audible volume, like a strong handshake, also conveys confidence.

I have noticed cultural differences in volume between Americans and some international students. If you are on the quieter side, it might require you to work harder to speak at the level of the prevalent cultural norms of US business. One semester, I mentored three female graduate students from China who were all working to land jobs at a variety of tech companies. We spent several of our get togethers practicing greeting each other with solid and friendly handshakes, making eye contact, smiling, and engaging in conversation at an audible and energetic level. All I can say is, practice, practice, and practice.

Exude confidence

Get proficient with these three basics. Practice with friends:

- » Greet with a handshake
- » Focus on making eye contact
- » Chat and make sure they don't have to strain to hear you

If you already have these three nailed, that's perfect.

Use your professors' office hours—seriously

Let me be clear, all this advice is from my current vantage. I didn't take all these actions when I was in school. That is especially true of getting to know professors and using their office hours. I can actually only remember two professors from undergrad. One was the famous lawyer/author/actor, Ben Stein. He was an adjunct professor teaching business law at Pepperdine. He is also the actor who plays the droll teacher in Ferris Bueller's Day Off who says "Bueller? Bueller?" The movie had just come out in 1986—so having him as a professor was pretty cool and very memorable.

The other professor I remember is from my semester in London. She was extremely passionate about

English literature. She would get so worked up. She loved it. And she talked for hours about it—hours and hours. Given London had a lower drinking age than the US, I was often very tired in her class from staying out in pubs and clubs. I would totally appreciate her passion now, at the time, I did not. One day leaving class, we were all crammed into an elevator. As the door shut, I exclaimed, "That was sooooo boring." The person next to me made crazy eyes at me pointing to the back of the elevator. The professor was in the back of the elevator. She was very gracious and tried to hide from me. I felt like a complete jerk. The next day I sucked it up and apologized to her before class. Again, she was gracious. It was a life lesson to not be a jerk. There were a few of those along the way.

Get to know your professors at their office hours, and this is especially true for adjunct professors who are also out in the working world. If you are getting As, go. If you are getting Bs, go. If you are getting Cs, go. Whatever you are getting, go. This is a great, low-risk, place to practice adulting with people who are there to help you grow as a person.

The people who spend time coming to my office hours, are the ones who I know really want to learn. I spend extra time with them—and that can help them produce stronger work. A number have kept the relationship going and ping me for periodic coffees. I've introduced some of them to contacts at companies hiring for positions. I care about their career progress.

Many professors also have access to cool research projects that would be amazing on your résumé. And they are the ones who can provide great perspective on majors and the related careers.

Presumably, you, or someone close to you is paying a lot for college. These professor relationships are included in the cost, but something which very few fully take advantage. Take advantage.

On a related note, start building a relationship with your academic advisor sometime during your freshman year. You want them to know who you are so their guidance can be more meaningful and relevant. Most advisors are busy people and see hundreds of students. You'll need to be diligent in getting time on a consistent basis, so they can remember who you are. If you can, avoid class registration time. Be patient and keep working to get scheduled—perhaps once a term.

Humanize your professors (yes, they are people too)

Find out when their office hours are—the class syllabus should tell you. Then take advantage—sometimes professors prefer you to pre-schedule over email and others are okay if you just drop in. Here are a few angles you can choose from to set up and anchor your discussion:

> » I'm struggling with INSERT HOMEWORK and was hoping to clarify a few things.
> » I'm a little unclear on INSERT TOPIC

from class today and was hoping to better understand it.

» I really enjoy your class and I'm thinking about being an INSERT MAJOR. Would you be willing to spend some time talking through the typical career paths for this choice?

Career: Getting started

Let's pivot to some career actions. This next section is a bit longer, but it should only take two to three hours of your time—the first action will take less than an hour.

Find the career center—make friends with somebody who works there

This is an easy one. Your school has a career center. Your job is to find it. Ask around. Some students never find it. You can be one of the few who take full advantage of the resources at their disposal. Do not wait.

This year the goal is to find it and make a friend. For the following three years, your job will be to understand the upcoming calendar of events for the career center. The key word is upcoming. It does you no good to know that the career fair, or the opportunity to do some mock interviews, was yesterday or last week. You need to know about key activities before they happen.

Check it out

Find the career center. Walk up to somebody that looks like they work there, introduce yourself as a new freshman—try out your handshake, eye-contact, and audible volume. <u>Make friends with this person.</u> Learn their name. Ask what actions they recommend you take as a freshman. Try out, "Tell me more." Or "What else?". Take their suggested actions. On this first visit, ask if your school has a professional mentor program. If they do, sign up.

> **Create a V1 résumé—identify your gaps so you can focus on filling them**

This one may take a couple of hours.

Not long ago, I interviewed a recent graduate for a marketing position. She was a marketing major with meaningful internships in the field of marketing in each of her three summer breaks. Three. She may, or may not, have had her grades on the résumé. I don't recall, however, she had lots of activities on her résumé and seemed interesting and hard working. Her résumé was very impressive for a recent graduate. She was articulate and confident to match how she showed up on paper. She knew what entry level roles were in marketing. She had a passion for <u>the field </u>that came through in our conversation. I was impressed.

That person is your competition. You can replace the word marketing in the previous paragraph with any major. Pretend it is your senior year and try it out below inserting the major you are currently thinking about.

I am a _____ major. I had meaningful internships in the field of _____ in several of my summer breaks. I have lots of activities on my résumé and seem interesting and hard working. My résumé is very impressive for a recent graduate. I am articulate and confident. I know what entry level roles are in _____. I have a passion for _____ that comes through to potential employers.

How did reading that feel? It's okay if it feels weird at this point. That's normal. Try it out with different majors you are pondering. Does one feel better than another? This gets back to my advice: be obsessively curious about majors and the related jobs. Let me just say, I have never seen somebody with three relevant summer internships before. She was an anomaly. I will also say, though, I went out of my way to find her a role.

The other point I made in the opening of this section is that I don't recall if her grades were on her résumé or not. I had no idea if she is an A student or not. Sure, some other potential employer may ask her about her grades, or care more about that, but the point is her résumé was impressive regardless of her classroom academics. It came through that she was interesting, passionate, and knowledgeable in marketing.

You may ask, why are we talking about all this in the résumé section? The person I met with was clearly intentional about how she spent her time in college.

We're creating your résumé now so that you can see your starting point, and then be intentional in building out your story.

Start with a template

Time to create your V1 résumé. The starting place can be a Microsoft Word or Google Docs template. The template should be clean and simple. You'll see a bunch that have bright colors and wacky borders. Don't pick one of those. Also, I have no idea why some of their default templates include photos—photos are not something generally included in résumés at least in the US. Unless you're applying for jobs in broadcasting or on-camera media, skip the photo.

Check out these free program templates that illustrate two basic formats.

Microsoft Word—One-column

WELL-BAKED PIE

Address · Phone
Email · LinkedIn Profile · Twitter/Blog/Portfolio

To replace this text with your own, just click it and start typing. Briefly state your career objective, or summarize what makes you stand out. Use language from the job description as keywords.

EXPERIENCE

DATES FROM – TO
JOB TITLE, COMPANY
Describe your responsibilities and achievements in terms of impact and results. Use examples, but keep it short.

DATES FROM – TO
JOB TITLE, COMPANY
Describe your responsibilities and achievements in terms of impact and results. Use examples, but keep it short.

EDUCATION

MONTH YEAR
DEGREE TITLE, SCHOOL
It's okay to brag about your GPA, awards, and honors. Feel free to summarize your coursework too.

MONTH YEAR
DEGREE TITLE, SCHOOL
It's okay to brag about your GPA, awards, and honors. Feel free to summarize your coursework too.

SKILLS

- List your strengths relevant for the role you're applying for
- List one of your strengths

- List one of your strengths
- List one of your strengths
- List one of your strengths

ACTIVITIES

Use this section to highlight your relevant passions, activities, and how you like to give back. It's good to include Leadership and volunteer experiences here. Or show off important extras like publications, certifications, languages and more.

Microsoft Word—Two-column

Well-Baked Pie
title

Contact

[Address]
[City, ST ZIP Code]
[Phone]
[Email]

Objective

[Replace this sentence with your job objective. To replace any tip text with your own, just select a line of text and start typing. For best results when selecting text to copy or replace, don't include space to the right of the characters in your selection.]

Education

[School Name],
[City], [State]
[You might want to include your GPA here and a brief summary of relevant coursework, awards, and honors.]

Experience

[Dates From] – [To]
[Job Title] • [Job Position] • [Company Name]

[Dates From] – [To]
[Job Title] • [Job Position] • [Company Name]

[Dates From] – [To]
[Job Title] • [Job Position] • [Company Name]

[This is the place for a brief summary of your key responsibilities and most stellar accomplishments.]

Key Skills

Marketing
Project Management
Budget Planning
Social Media
Planning

Communication

[You delivered that big presentation to rave reviews. Don't be shy about it now!
This is the place to show how well you work and play with others.]

Leadership

[Are you president of your fraternity, head of the condo board, or a team lead for your favorite charity?
You're a natural leader—tell it like it is!]

References

[Available upon request.]

The two basic formats are one-column or two-column. I know my preference, but I did some polling to see what other recruiters and hiring managers prefer to see. Honestly, the feedback was mixed and all over the place. There was probably a minor leaning toward one-column. That said, I recommend the two-column format for early career because there is less real estate to fill with job experience and the page can be more visually impactful with college activities, awards, leadership, and skills. Ask your career center friend what they think and feel free to take their advice or mine—it's a gray area.

In my poll on column preference, there was one comment that I thought summed it up well. "I don't care about the columns, I just want it to be easy to navigate and scan." Said another way, make sure there is some healthy whitespace on your résumé. Also, it should only be one page—now, and probably for a good number of years into your career.

For a small cost, you can start with an even better designed template.

Another area I polled on was how much design mattered in relation to content. I'll net it out for you. Good visual design matters. It communicates attention to detail. It communicates polish. Over design though, is also not good. By over design, I mean lots of colors, too many icons, photos, and super unique layouts.

Etsy is a great place to find résumé templates that are a step up in design from the free templates.

Check out the example that I downloaded for less than ten dollars.

Default Template

WELL-BAKED PIE

POSITION TITLE

 000 – 123 – 456

 youremail@mail.com

 Jacksonville, FL

 Linkedinprofilelink

PROFESSIONAL PROFILE

Lorem ipsum is simply dummy text of the printing and typesetting industry. lorem ipsum has been the industry's standard dummy text ever since the 1500s, when an unknown printer took a galley of type and scrambled it to make a type specimen book. It has survived not only five centuries, but also the leap into electronic typesetting,

EDUCATION

DEGREE NAME // MAJOR
University, Location
2007-2012

DEGREE NAME // MAJOR
University, Location
2008-2010

SKILLS

PROFESSIONAL

New Business Development
Territory Expansion

Executive Presentations

Competitive Market Positioning

Account Management

Client Needs Assessment

Executive Presentations

Client Needs Assessment

WORK EXPERIENCE

WRITE YOUR JOB TITLE HERE
Company Name | Location | 2012 – Present

Lorem Ipsum is simply dummy text of the printing and typesetting industry. Lorem Ipsum has been the industry's standard dummy text ever since the 1500s, when an unknown printer took
- Lorem Ipsum is simply dummy text of the printing and typeset
- Lorem Ipsum is simply dummy text of the printing and typeset
- Lorem Ipsum is simply dummy text of the printing and typeset

WRITE YOUR JOB TITLE HERE
Company Name | Location | 2012 – Present

Lorem Ipsum is simply dummy text of the printing and typesetting industry. Lorem Ipsum has been the industry's standard dummy text ever since the 1500s, when an unknown printer took
- Lorem Ipsum is simply dummy text of the printing and typeset
- Lorem Ipsum is simply dummy text of the printing and typeset
- Lorem Ipsum is simply dummy text of the printing and typeset

WRITE YOUR JOB TITLE HERE
Company Name | Location | 2012 – Present

Lorem Ipsum is simply dummy text of the printing and typesetting industry. Lorem Ipsum has been the industry's standard dummy text ever since the
- Lorem Ipsum is simply dummy text of the printing and typeset
- Lorem Ipsum is simply dummy text of the printing and typeset
- Lorem Ipsum is simply dummy text of the printing and typeset

It is clean and simple, but it conveys a maturity and polish that the base Word and Google templates do not. If you do use an Etsy template, be sure to download and install any necessary fonts to have the template render correctly—and always turn it into a PDF so it renders for others the same way that it does for you. I was left confident that the résumé scanning tools that companies use today work just as well with PDFs as native files like Word and Google.

Add sections to the template to make the most of your strengths.

Make the most of your content by customizing what sections are on your version of the template.

Customized Example

WELL-BAKED PIE

P O S I T I O N   T I T L E

000 – 123 – 456

youremail@mail.com

Jacksonville, FL

Linkedinprofilelink

PROFESSIONAL PROFILE

Lorem ipsum is simply dummy text of the printing and typesetting industry. lorem ipsum has been the industry's standard dummy text ever since the 1500s, when an unknown printer took a galley of type and scrambled it to make a type specimen book. It has survived not only five centuries, but also the leap into electronic typesetting.

EDUCATION

DEGREE NAME // MAJOR
University, Location
2007-2012

Semester Abroad
Location
2008

SKILLS

New Business Development
Territory Expansion

Executive Presentations

Competitive Market Positioning

Account Management

ACTIVITIES

Ski Club

Debate Team

Theatre Stage Crew

WORK EXPERIENCE

WRITE YOUR JOB TITLE HERE
Company Name | Location | 2012 – Present

Lorem Ipsum is simply dummy text of the printing and typesetting industry. Lorem Ipsum has been the industry's standard dummy text
- Lorem Ipsum is simply dummy text of the printing and typeset
- Lorem Ipsum is simply dummy text of the printing and typeset

WRITE YOUR JOB TITLE HERE
Company Name | Location | 2012 – Present

Lorem Ipsum is simply dummy text of the printing and typesetting industry. Lorem Ipsum has been the industry's standard dummy text
- Lorem Ipsum is simply dummy text of the printing and typeset
- Lorem Ipsum is simply dummy text of the printing and typeset

VOLUNTEERING

WRITE ACTIVITY HERE
Non-profit | Location | 2012 – Present

Lorem Ipsum is simply dummy text of the printing and typesetting industry. Lorem Ipsum has been the industry's standard dummy text

WRITE ACTIVITY HERE
Non-profit | Location | 2012 – Present

Lorem Ipsum is simply dummy text of the printing and typesetting industry. Lorem Ipsum has been the industry's standard dummy text

The bold boxes highlight new content and sections that could be added to this template to better communicate value beyond just work experience. I added an Activities section versus having just Skills on the left. If applicable, an Awards section could also be added. On the bottom right there is now a section for Volunteering. This could instead be titled Leadership if you have more content that fits under that descriptive header. Use your judgment on what sections make most sense to customize based on the content you have to highlight.

You can also see how doing a semester abroad (one of my recommendations) adds more meat to the Education section.

In the future, position title will become your target role.

Don't sweat the position title and professional profile section content too much for now. This content will evolve as you figure out more about your major and the roles you will be trying to land, as well as the skills and highlights you bring to bear. We'll deal with these sections more as you work to land summer internships after your sophomore and junior years.

Make the most of your part-time and summer jobs.

I'm hoping you had a job or two in high school. You'll want to make the most of how you describe those jobs as well as the jobs you hold during college. What do I mean by that? I mean, think hard about the responsibilities and skills you used, regardless of the job, and don't undersell them. Don't go overboard either. Give some detail so that employers can envision you being responsible and, as much as the jobs permit, exhibiting work traits they would likely value. Let's look at two job examples and what underselling looks like compared to the right level of illustrative detail.

Fast Food Cashier
Undersell
Cashier

On target
Engaged customers and supported restaurant operations—cashiered, served food, opened/closed, and stocked inventory.

Babysitter
Undersell
Babysitter

On target
Watched over two children ages three and seven for twenty hours a week. Responsibilities included driving the children to/from activities, reading books together, and finding other creative ways to entertain.

You want to use language that illustrates you being responsible and hardworking. We'll cover this in more detail in a later section.

Throughout college, you'll swap out high school content for college.

Upon graduation, employers will not be focused on activities, volunteering, or leadership that you had in high school. Over the four years, you'll need to swap out the high school content with college content. That is why it is so important to be purposeful on what you get involved in during college so that you can be perceived as a well-rounded go-getter—both for summer internships and full-time roles.

Important rant—you must proofread.

Do not use improper grammar, misspell, or have typos on your résumé. Proofread! Proofread! Proofread! Then have someone else proofread.

Find your résumé gaps

Create your résumé in a visually appealing template where your content can come to life over the coming years.

While this was a longer section, it should take only a couple hours to complete this first version of your résumé. Summary steps:

> » Pick out your template—Etsy is a great place to start

» Fill it in to best of your ability—adding sections as relevant
» Proofread it
» Proofread it again
» Have somebody else proofread it
» Note where you want/need to have more content a couple years from now
» Get a plan for how you will fill in the holes

Reminder: whenever you send your résumé to others, always send it as a PDF to ensure your formatting is viewed correctly. If you send in the native format with a custom font, and the recipient doesn't have that font, the formatting will be off.

Freshman second-term recap

Freshman year. Check. How did you do? You on your way to becoming somebody employers will get excited about? If you missed taking any of the below actions, you have the summer, and can always revisit them next fall.

Heart: Defining your passion

» Doubled down on curiosity and adopted "Tell me more." and "What else?"

Social: Developing soft skills

» Learned about semester abroad and figured out if it is feasible.
» Nailed handshake, eye contact, and volume.
» Met with at least one professor and dug in with some curiosity.

Career: Getting started

» Found the career center and made a friend.
» Created my V1 résumé and identified some content holes I'd like to work on.

Please set a reminder to dive into *A Well–Baked Pie* about a month out from heading back to school.

SOPHOMORE YEAR

Apply some more rigor to your adulting

One year down, three to go. You have plenty of time. Relax. Take it easy. Kick back. I wish that was my advice but, sadly, it is not. In reality, your sophomore year requires getting more serious on the job front. I've still laid out what you need to do in easy-to-follow steps. So, there is no need to get stressed out. You just need to be purposeful and intentional in making time to take the actions.

Heart: Homing in

In this heart section, I'll start with a little reality check. I'll also continue on the theme of curiosity, but with a bit more emphasis toward landing the plane around your major—or at least finding the airport.

Get your shit together: Real life is coming in hot

I started the freshman year section with two lists. One of those lists included Mario Kart, sleeping all day, binge drinking, puking, and more. We could call it fun pie. Let's call it for what it is at this point—the I'm-on-my-way-to-flunking-out pie. During your freshman year, if you participated in more activities from that first list than my other list, your sophomore year is the time to get a grip. Real life is coming in hot, and the transition time to adjust to college is now over. Also, you may think you are messing with your parents. Not true. This is your life, not theirs. You are messing with yourself.

Remember the seven ingredient areas for growing as a whole person. Work on each one.

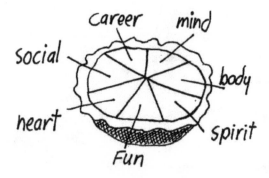

Get in the game

Invest in yourself. Your action is to look yourself in the mirror and honestly say you are investing in your life and taking the actions below. If you can't, figure out what you need to do to get out of your own way. You're steering the ship at this point, not your parents—and the ship is your life.

- » Studying and going to class
- » Being curious about majors and the typical jobs that align to majors
- » Trying new activities and getting leadership positions
- » Meeting new people and growing your network
- » Morphing from a young adult to a young professional
- » Being active and exercising
- » Getting work experience—for life skills and your résumé

If you started out working hard on the list above—major props. Keep it up. Seriously, that's impressive. Check the box for this and move on.

Aggressively ponder your major—ideally pick something during your fall term

My hope is that you spent a lot of time your freshman year being obsessively curious about majors. That curiosity and uncertainty may continue into your sophomore year. It is still definitely okay to be in somewhat of an exploratory mode, but not for much longer if you want to finish in four years. I would encourage switching from obsessively curious to aggressively pondering.

Obsessively Curious → **Aggressively Pondering**

What do I mean by aggressively pondering? Start to create pro and con lists. Start to really dig into a day in the life of typical jobs that result from the different options. Start to trust your gut. If you change majors during the latter part of your sophomore year, you may need to add semesters/quarters to get all the credits you need for your new major. Keep an active relationship going with your academic advisor to understand the implications of changing majors in terms of either added course load or additional semesters/quarters.

I said it in the opening of the book: Your major is not a life sentence. In the business world, most of the time (and I mean 95 percent or more) majors are not even something that comes up after that first job unless you're in a highly specialized professional field such as architecture or electronical engineering. I have no idea what any of the majors are of the plethora of successful people I work with every day.

Circle the airport...and get your eyes on a runway

Aggressively ponder. If you aren't yet feeling solid about your choice of major, get with your academic advisor early in the fall. Discuss the various majors you have been exploring and fully understand the implications of each on your academic choices. Talk to your parents or any adult mentors you have. You may not be quite ready to land the plane on this, but you should be at least circling the airport and perhaps even be eyeing the runway.

Social: Adulting your communications

Here is where we are going to start doing some heavy lifting toward adulting. While graduation and having a job may feel a long way off, if you're on the right path, this is the year you will start to interact with working professionals. I have some additional advice to keep moving the needle on how you can show up and impress in your social interactions.

Every conversation is an opportunity to impress.

The truth is we live in a world where first impressions happen whether we like it or not. Knowing this, let's take a moment to set the stage and talk about the working professionals you will come in contact with over the next three years. They will range in age. They will range in their level of casualness and formality. They will range in their expectations for professional communication. They will range in how fast they assess you.

For purposes of painting a picture, I'm going to use myself as somebody you could come across. If you prepare for me, others should be easier. I'm older (which means I have high standards for written communications), casual and friendly in how I present in person, and I have a high bar for candidates. I'm friendly and warm when in contact with job candidates. I'm smiling. I'm working to put you at ease. I'm actively engaged in the conversation. You would probably leave a conversation with me and think, "Wow, that went great."

And it might have felt great from an interaction standpoint, but I am assessing on whether I want to hire you, refer you to a hiring manager, or invest my time helping you in your career because I see potential. And I'm assessing you within the first minute. Even faster. I can't help it. I looked it up and some scientists say people start to form impressions of a person after seeing their face for less than one-tenth of a second. In that time, people can decide whether or not the person is "attractive, trustworthy, competent, extroverted, or dominant." Dang. That's fast.

And if you don't make a good impression in those first moments, it will be hard for you to change impressions—possible, but hard. I try not to assess too quickly, but the reality is that I do. And so do many others. Let me tell you what I take in within the first minute of meeting you. If you:

» Have a strong handshake that is not sweaty or odd
» Have clean looking hair
» Have clean eyeglasses
» Make eye contact
» Have clean teeth
» Have clothes that fit you and are clean and pressed
» Have polished your shoes
» Have an overall put-together look
» Have confident posture
» Appear energetic
» Speak fluidly, avoiding vocal fry or filler words (also known as Kardashian-like)
» Appear confident without going over the edge to arrogant

That's a lot of stuff for one minute. I don't consciously go through that list. I just know that is what my brain takes in. Try it yourself as you meet new people. You may find you do the same thing. I could write you off as a candidate for any one shortcoming but I'm quickly putting all those details together to tell myself a story about you. Over the coming three years, the advice in these social sections will build out your skills so you can show up strong. We already went over handshakes, eye-contact, and speaking volume. Now let's cover some more professional fundamentals under the theme of applying more rigor to your adulting—and reducing the gap between student and working professional.

> ## Start building the muscle for professional email communications—concise and clear

Email is generally a predecessor to in-person communication, so let's start there. I love efficient communications. In my internal work emails, I can't even be bothered to type my full name, I use "b." I can't be bothered to type the "rian" to finish it off as it slows me down. That said, when I am interacting with a new client, I use the full "Brian." I adjust based on the circumstance and the formality required.

Texting is very efficient. You becomes U; just kidding becomes JK. Okay becomes K or KK—I have recently come to learn that K means I am not necessarily pleased. You grew up in a world of texting with shortened words, partial sentences, and no punctuation. I love that efficiency, but you need to be able to compose professional emails that use sentences, punctuation, and are:

» Concise
» Clear
» Passionate/energetic
» Appreciative
» Professional

Let's look at an example and then I'll break it down. It is a scenario where you are communicating over LinkedIn with a recent alum of your university—one working in a role you would love to have after graduation. We'll cover networking coffees later in the book.

> *Hello Mary,*
>
> *I'm in ABC University class of 202X and you have my post-graduation dream job. Would you be open to my buying you coffee so I can ask questions about the role and how you landed it? I'd love to make sure I am taking similar steps. Are there some options that work the week of X/X? I would be very happy to come to you.*
>
> *I really appreciate you considering this. Thank you so much!*
>
> *Best,*
>
> *Brian*

Let's break that down. First, I need to emphasize that am purposefully using the word professional, not formal. You will see I did not use "Dear." I personally think it seems somewhat antiquated. There are those that would argue against me, and I don't feel strongly. Do what makes you comfortable.

I also used the person's first name. There are some who might argue for Mr., Mrs., and Ms. I would argue harder, use first name unless you are addressing a person who is much older and has a lot of academic credentials. Those people tend to like Dear Dr. So-and-So.

Let's dissect that email against the five criteria:

» Concise—It is seven sentences, yet still friendly and provides enough context.

» Clear—It communicates who I am, the university connection we share, what I hope to talk about, why I want to discuss that, and a specific ask around time.

» Passionate/Energetic—It uses language to convey passion and energy, for example "dream job," "love to," and "very happy."

» Appreciative—Two of the seven sentences are used to express appreciation.

» Professional—Finally, it uses full sentences and punctuation.

For closing emails, "sincerely yours" and "sincerely" seem from the days of yore. I like these:

> *Best,*
> *Warmly,*
> *Thank you!*

A real example

After I wrote the above section, I was on a career panel for undergrads—the panel was a mix of recruiters and hiring managers. When I was leaving, a student stopped me to talk about consulting. I had to run so I encouraged him to connect with me on LinkedIn. Check out the verbatim note (last name removed) he sent me early the next morning. It was kind of spooky how close he was to my directions. I was impressed.

> *Hi Brian,*
>
> *My name is FIRSTNAME LASTNAME and I am a first-year Finance student with junior standing. We spoke briefly after you came in as a guest speaker for the career lunch and learn. I would love to learn a bit more about the consulting industry and your other professional experiences. Would you be willing to chat over some coffee? If so, could you please let me know your schedule, so I can work around it.*
>
> *Once again thank you for your time.*
> *Best,*
> *FIRSTNAME LASTNAME*

Only three students of the thirty present came up to any of us after the panel. Wasted opportunity. Take advantage of speaking to professionals who have taken the time to come to your campus and educate you on how to land a job with their company. The chances are those people are pretty darn friendly as well as understanding of your situation. Practice the art of conversation and possibly learn something, or make a contact, to help you later in your job search process.

Downsides of snail mail

On a related communication side note: use email for professional correspondence, not the postal mail. I have had people I interview send me thank you cards through the mail. That is a nice gesture but, by the time I receive their note, we have typically already made the hiring decision. Also, when multiple people interview someone, we can forward around a thank you email—especially one that shows passion for the job and gets us excited about hiring the candidate. We cannot do that with a hand-written note.

I have heard of candidates leaving, walking outside, completing a hand-written card, and walking back in to deliver it. In general, hand-written cards are nice. That said, this approach won't win every person over. My preferences is you take a bit more time and compose a strong email that you send later that day.

Build your muscle

Practice applying the five criteria when you communicate and then ask yourself the following. I mean it, really ask yourself these questions:

> » Am I using extra words or sentences?
> » Is my purpose and/or ask clear and simple?
> » Do I sound passionate?
> » Do I express appreciation?
> » Have I used proper punctuation?

When sending important emails to new contacts in your network, or as a follow up to a conversation or interview, run them by someone that you trust. Ask for feedback to make it more clear and concise.

Keep evolving how you show up—like, stop... um...using filler words

Verbal interaction requires thought, just as written communication does. If this one is not an issue for you, great. Consider yourself lucky and move on.

Stop using filler words.

I've said several things are easy. Breaking the habit of filler words is not. If you use filler words, you may not believe it, but in the eyes of a prospective employer, they reduce your IQ. Like, you know, I mean, a lot. Like, I um, don't, ah, even like want to like, have like, sort of a conversation with you. Like, I'm serious.

See how hard that was to follow? My display of ignorance could not be missed. We've all heard people who sound like that, even on National Public Radio. When groups of people live together, they pick up speech patterns from each other. If these brutal-to-listen-to-IQ-reducing speech patterns exist within your college friend group, pick one friend and start calling each other out to help break the filler-word habit.

My daughter and I were recently at a coffee shop sitting next to a girl from a sorority talking to her friend about another friend that had wronged her. Oh guurrl, her friend was sooo baaad. We didn't mean to eavesdrop, but she was very loud and also, very entertaining. She had so many variations of using the word like, and other IQ-reducing language, that I started texting each unique one to my daughter. Here is the list.

- » You know
- » I mean
- » Like
- » Literally
- » I'm like
- » I was like
- » Oh my God
- » You know what
  I mean

- » And I'm like
- » I know right
- » Shuuut uuuup
- » So it's like
- » And like
- » Just like
- » Whereas like

My favorite was "whereas like." You have to appreciate the juxtaposition of the formality of "whereas" with "like." Beyond "like," the other words I would become conscious about using too much are:

- » So
- » Uh
- » Um
- » Ahh
- » I mean

- » You know
- » Sort of
- » Kind of
- » Kinda

Uptalk and vocal fry frequently accompany filler words. If your statements sound like questions, you'll also need to fix that. (In all fairness, ending a statement as though it were a question can be a regionalism rather than an age-specific copycat speech pattern. Regardless of the reason, identify the issue and address it.)

Become aware

How do you fix these things? The first step is to become aware. I recommend you hit the audio record on your phone during a few conversations and listen back. If you can, record yourself having both casual conversations with friends as well as more formal conversations where you may be feeling a little nervous. Understanding your default fillers or vocal behaviors is the starting point for change. My main fillers have historically been "um" and "so, uh."

Slow down and pause

Start catching yourself. Slowdown in your conversations and pause where you would normally stick a filler word. Do this over the course of weeks until you have killed the filler words. At the start of working on this it will be difficult to speak at all. As you catch yourself, pause and try again.

If you are still struggling after working on this for a while, enlist a friend or two. Try this:

» Ask them if they are willing to help you improve some of your speech habits.
» Tell them what you are working on and agree on a signal they can use when they hear it.
» Become more aware and start catching and correcting yourself.
» Periodically record yourself in conversation to check your progress.
» Be patient.

Like, stop

Break the habit. Again, if you have a habit of using filler words, it will be hard to break it. You must break it though and you'll need persistence, and perhaps a friend or parent to help you.

> **Learn three conversation (aka interview) habits—preparation, curiosity, and follow-up**

Let me start by reinforcing, any conversation with people in the working world could/should also be considered an interview. If you appear buttoned up, intelligent, and hungry, people are going to want to help you—whether it is an official interview or not. We've already covered some basics for conversations: strong handshake, eye contact, audible volume, and elimination of filler words. Let's build on that with a three-habit framework for conversation.

#1 Prepare—it does wonders for your confidence

There is a great quote from Benjamin Franklin, "By failing to prepare, you are preparing to fail." I can't say it better. Prepare for any conversation you are going to have. It depends on the situation, but in general, preparation related to career conversations happens at three levels:

Company
Position
Person

You won't always be interacting about a specific position, but you'll always want to be aware of some detail about the person and the company where they work.

Preparation basics:

Company

> » Explore their website—especially learning about what they do and what they value in their corporate culture and employees
>
> » Explore Glassdoor—see how they are rated and get a vibe for what people think about working there
>
> » Search "recent news about COMPANY"
>
> » Talk to people you know that work there
>
> » Explore competitor websites—see if there are any interesting contrasts on how they appear

Position

> » Thoroughly read the job description for anything for which you are applying—print it and highlight what's most important (and keep it for reference if you do make it to interviews)
>
> » Talk to people you may know working in a similar role

Person

> » Read their LinkedIn profile and look for any commonalities you might be able to bring up in conversation

» Look at their skills, groups they belong to or feedback from others to identify things they're good at or interested in—to possibly ask about when you talk

» Talk to any people you know in common—try to get a pulse on their personality

#2 Be curious and enthusiastic

Over time, you won't have to worry about your handshake, eye contact, filler words, and audible volume. If you aren't there yet, think about those basics. Preparation reduces anxiety. With your anxiety reduced, you can focus on showing up to conversations curious and enthusiastic. For me, enthusiasm encompasses both smiling and bringing energy. Curiosity and enthusiasm will get you far in creating successful conversations.

Curiosity is about having a mindset of learning. The questions you ask will vary depending upon the exact purpose of your conversation, but here are some illustrative questions that are broadly applicable. In any conversation, you are trying to convey that you prepared, and are enthusiastic and passionate to learn more.

Curiosity—illustrative questions:

Company

» How would you describe the culture?

» What are the traits of people who most excel?

» What do you think the big challenges will be for COMPANY over the next year or two?

Position

> » Can you give an example of a typical day?
> » What are some of the typical challenges in the role?
> » What would success look like in thirty days? Ninety? One year?
> » How does this role fit into the whole department?
> » What are some of the best classes that prepare you for this role?

Person

> » What was your path coming out of college?
> » What skills do you think are most important in your role?
> » What are some recent things you worked on in your role?
> » What are some of your key goals in the coming year?

#3 Follow up—with appreciation and clarity on any agreements

Always follow up via email! Get an email out the same day expressing your appreciation for the meeting. You should also clarify any agreed actions—whether they are yours or the other person's actions. Here is another email example that is concise, clear, passionate, appreciative, and professional. Notice that I included a specific detail about the conversation and the impact it had on me.

> Mary,
>
> Thank you so much for talking with me. I enjoyed learning about your career journey and your perspective makes me feel more confident about my path.
>
> I have attached my résumé. Thank you so much for offering to forward it to NAME, at COMPANY.
>
> I really appreciate your help.
> Best,
> Brian

On a related note, once you start interacting with those in the working world, **you will need to check your email at least once a day**. Seriously. Two times a day is better. Being responsive is an important trait when job hunting.

And, on another related note to communication channels, make sure your voicemail is set up. Unlike your friends, professionals will not be Snapchatting or texting you. They will be emailing or calling. Take five minutes right now to record a new outgoing message. Put some energy in your voice. Make it your own, but something along the lines of:

"Hi. You've reached Brian Ladyman. Your call is important, and I will follow up as soon as I can. Thank you and have an amazing day!"

Now do it again with more energy. Call from another phone and listen to it. One more time? Do you sound like an enthusiastic and energetic future employee?

Become a conversation machine

You need to create three habits around conversations (aka interviews):

» Prepare
» Be curious and enthusiastic
» Follow up through email

Attack career fairs—be hungry, you're being interviewed

Fairs are fun. There are rides, and animals, and lots of places to get great tasting and terrible-for-you food (for example, funnel cake, corn dogs, and pretty much anything you can throw in a fryer). Surely a career fair will be similarly festive and fun. Right? Wrong—no rides, animals, food, or fun. That said, it can be an energizing day if you go into it with the right attitude and expectations.

So, let me set expectations for the typical career fair. There will be a big room with lots of different employers in small booths or at tables. Some of the employers will have long lines of students, others will have none and be desperate for students to stop by and talk to them. Many times, it is as awkward and draining a day for the employers as it is for students. Like the students, employers need to "be on" too. Employers are looking for some great, stand-out candidates, but will spend the day interacting with students on the full spectrum of interest to them—including students that can barely hold a conversation. Your goal is to be a bright spot in their day.

I purposely chose the word attack versus attend. Attend is passive. Attack is aggressive. Attend means you show up and wander aimlessly around. Attack means you have a plan and go hard. Attack. Don't attend.

Do a little prep (I hope you notice that preparation is a theme.)

Your preparation goal is to make the most of your time at the career fair and have a fledgling of an idea of what each company does before you talk to them. You do not want to start conversations with, "So what does COMPANY X do?" That is not being a bright spot in their day. Don't ask questions that can easily be found on the company website.

A few days before the career fair, visit your friend at the career center (remember the one you made freshman year). Ask if you can see the list of companies planning to attend the career fair. Then remind him/her of your current major and ask which four to five companies they would recommend you focus on engaging in conversation. Those recommendations are a great starting point.

Then fire up your computer—or just look at your phone—and get to know a little bit about the four to five companies. I'd say spend at least fifteen to twenty minutes on each company taking these actions noted previously:

» Explore their website
» Explore Glassdoor
» Search "recent news about COMPANY"
» Talk to people you know that work there (if you have time)

That should do it. This level of research should give you a feel for how the company represents themselves, what employees think, and provide any news hooks that, if the opportunity arises, will allow you to show that you did some research. It also should give you enough to be able to authentically engage from a position of curiosity.

Get groomed

I wish this section wasn't necessary. I really do. Unfortunately, I have experienced that it is. Before the day of the career fair, be sure you have had a decent haircut and, if needed, removed any scruffy facial hair. On the day, shower, groom your hair, floss your teeth, and also brush them—you will be in close talking distance to people. If you wear glasses, clean them. I can't tell you how many people I have talked to having to connect through the grime on their glasses. Grime is not impressive. You'll also want to put on your best business outfit (more on that in the next section).

Today you are not trying to impress your friends by how unkempt you are or how cool you look in your beanie or yoga pants. You are trying to impress prospective employers on how polished and adult you are. As a sophomore, it may feel strange. That's okay. Go with it. Fake it 'til you make it as they say.

Have a strategy and show up curious and enthusiastic

On the day of the career fair, you need a plan. The most popular employer booths will grow long lines as the day goes on. You'll need to be prepared to stand in line with patience and a smile. The following strategy is designed to help you minimize time waiting in lines and gives you some conversation warm up time by having you talk first to companies where you are not necessarily interested to land a job. I recommend:

» Show up as early as you can as the lines grow over time.

» Start by talking to four to five organizations that are *not on* your target list—get some jitters out and perhaps stumble across something amazing.

» Visit your target companies, non-profits, government agencies, and branches of the military—engage in conversation with curiosity and enthusiasm. Be sure to get a business card and take notes on each conversation immediately after.

» Feel free to wander around the fair after those conversations, or just go relax because you did what you came to do.

» Follow up where you have interest—connect on

LinkedIn and send a message referencing any highlights from the conversation.

» Start the conversation with an introduction—including your name and year of graduation

A career fair is just a unique instance of conversation. The three conversation habits we just covered totally apply.

1. Prepare
2. Be curious and enthusiastic
3. Follow up through email (or LinkedIn if you forget to get a business card)

In the case of talking to an employer representative at a career fair booth, I would encourage you to shake hands (or read the cues on what greeting type they are offering), introduce yourself, and state a short purpose. Your purpose as a sophomore is different than it is as a senior and you'll want to make that clear. Here is an example conversation opening with some personal connection and a pretty quick transition to your purpose.

Good morning. I'm Brian Ladyman and I'm a sophomore majoring in MAJOR. What's your name? (Unless they have a name tag on, in which case, you already know the name because your glasses are clean.)

I'm NAME.

Hi NAME. Nice to meet you. How's the day going so far?

Pretty good, we've been very busy.

I'm sure you have. COMPANY has a lot of buzz on campus. Thanks for taking a few minutes with me.

Absolutely.

I'm spending time learning more about a few companies that I'm interested in as possibilities for both internships and full-time roles after graduation. Would you be able to answer a few questions?

Sure.

Your questions could then include things from the previous conversation section. Engage in a curiosity-driven conversation. As you feel the conversation winding down, transition to close it down. Express your appreciation for their time and be clear on the follow up steps you will take. This following example assumes there is a summer internship possibility.

Thank you so much for taking the time with me. It really helped broaden my understanding beyond what I read online.

Of course. I think you could be a great fit.

I appreciate that. Before I leave, do you have a business card?

Sure. Here you go.

I'll connect with you on LinkedIn and send you my résumé. I'll remind you in the email that I'm the one who INSERT SOMETHING INTERESTING ABOUT YOU OR THE CONVERSATION.

Sounds great.

Enjoy the rest of your day!

Take notes on your conversations

This will not be your last career fair. You might run into these exact same people next year. Seriously. After you leave a conversation, take five minutes to write down or type some notes. You will be so happy you have these to refer to as you prepare for future career fairs. Jot down things like:

- » Names of people
- » Any personal information you learned (for example, how long they were at the company, position, if they are alumni or not, things you had in common, etc.)
- » Things you recall about the company
- » Things you recall they look for in their candidates
- » Any advice you received
- » Any follow up you discussed

These notes will also be helpful when you are doing your follow up. Trust me, if you don't take notes, all the conversations will blend together, and you won't remember who said what and what you promised for follow up.

Ride the rides

Career fairs are an amazing opportunity to learn and network in an efficient way. Make the most of them. If you sniff out a summer internship opportunity from your first visit to a career fair, think of it as an amazing bonus on top of the benefit of growing your conversational skills. If you don't, no worries. Ride the rides.

> » Prepare
> » Get groomed
> » Engage your strategy
> » Show up as early as you can
> » Start by talking to four to five companies that are *not* your target list
> » Visit your target companies—engage with curiosity and enthusiasm and then take notes
> » Follow up where you have interest

Career: Looking the part

Shifting from social skills and interaction, let's explore some tactical fundamentals that help you look the part of a driven and polished professional—both in person and digitally. The first action helps illustrate your drive. Then we'll dig into exactly what you'll need to put together a polished look that leaves you feeling confident and ready to talk business. And we'll get your digital presence ready to roll—LinkedIn and Handshake.

Get a job—even if it's just five to ten hours a week

You may have had jobs in high school. You may not have. Either way, whether you need to financially, or not, get a job during college at some point. If you are on work study, you may have started a job your freshman year. Regardless of what the job is, you will benefit in many career-related ways:

» Providing additional content for your résumé— messaging to future employers that you are driven, work hard, and can multi-task

» Learning more about what you like and don't like to do

» Gaining practical work and communication skills

» Having extra cash

There are generally a ton of jobs on campus with a variety of time commitments. Figure out what works for you. When I was a Pepperdine undergrad, I worked as a photographer for the school newspaper—taking and developing photos on my own time. I was into photography and it has remained a lifelong passion. I also have a friend—now a publishing professional—who went to a professor she heard was writing a book. She told him she was an aspiring writer and asked him if she could assist by transcribing and editing notes. He hired her for a semester's worth of work; it looked great on her résumé.

If it helps, think of your job like a class with no homework. One final note, if you do get a job and find you can't juggle everything, deprioritize the job.

Work

Get a job—maybe now, maybe later. That's it.

> **Get at least one business outfit—you're going to need it this year and beyond**

Depending upon where you live, this might be an action for the summer before you go back to school. For example, my daughter has many more options when home in Seattle than she does in Pullman, WA.

Why do you need a professional outfit as a sophomore? If for no other reason, the career fair. You will also be meeting with prospective employers from here onward. While interactions with visiting companies seem like they are just places for you to learn, they are not. Anyone you talk to is potentially interviewing you—so you need to look sharp and professional.

A business outfit is not something you party in

So, what is a business outfit? Let's talk about what it is not first. For men, it is not a dingy wrinkled shirt that look like it started out white but is now sort of a weird gray or cream color. It is not a suit that is awkwardly too small or too large. It is not white socks. For women, it is not the dress you wore dancing on Saturday night. It is not your fraternity-party pumps. It is also not necessarily an outfit that makes you look like a stereotypical tax accountant.

A business outfit is also not a uniform where everyone is wearing a navy suit and white shirt/blouse. Navy is an awesome staple when you only have one suit. That said, your style should help you stand out, not blend in with everyone else. If you go with a navy suit, make sure the rest of the outfit has some aspect that helps you stand out. If you stray from a navy suit, I wouldn't stray too far unless you're really confident in your style game—maybe charcoal gray, gray, black, or some other blue variation.

Buy something age-appropriate—but pretend your age is twenty-five

I imagine there is a big delta between what you wore when you were a sophomore in high school to what you wear now. That's four years. Well, four years from now what you will wear in your first year of work will be much different than what you wear today. It might be hard for you to fully grok (look it up it is a good word) what somebody in their early and mid-twenties wears. So, I recommend you go to a store and ask a sales person for help. Tell them, "I'm looking for an interview outfit that somebody in their mid-twenties would wear to a job interview. I want it to be professional, but also communicate that I have some style. Can you please put together some potential outfits for me?" See shopping list below.

Consider your location and target industry

Location and industry are two important aspects that come into play. The West Coast is more casual, as are industries like technology, advertising, and retail. On the more formal end, you have New York, Chicago, and industries like banking, law, and management consulting. When buying your base outfit(s), you'll want to understand which way your target location and industries generally lean and shop accordingly. You can always adjust your outfit to appear as a culture fit during interviews (for example, drop the tie to appear less formal). Pro tip: feel free to ask the recruiter about appropriate interview attire and/or ask anyone you know what managers typically wear.

Jumpstart your style

Here's a shopping list. If you already have some of these items, that's awesome. Just do a double check to ensure they aren't dingy, worn, or perhaps aren't quite right for interviewing. As a reminder, ask for help from a sales professional in the store. You'll want at least two outfits, so you can show up looking snazzy at both your initial and final interviews. That doesn't mean you need two suits, but it does mean you'll need more than one shirt/blouse and some tie and accessory options.

Shopping list:

Everyone and Anyone
» Suit
» Shirt/Blouse (two)
» Shoes
» Watch (optional)

He
» Tie (two)
» Belt
» White crew t-shirt
» Dark socks
» Pocket square (optional)
» Tie-clip (optional)

She
» Accessories/jewelry

The outfits you put together should make you feel confident. You should feel like you walk tall. You should feel like you can conquer the world. That confidence will come through as you are talking to potential employers. Remember, you are trying to balance professional business norms with some of your own style. Here are just a few final things to consider:

- » Suit—Tailored and fits well based on body type.
- » Dress Shirt—Measured to fit both neck and arm length.
- » Blouse—Generally subtle to complement the suit.
- » Tie—Not too narrow or too wide.
- » Pocket square—Optional and should complement the look.
- » Belt—General rule is same color as shoes.
- » Socks—Navy, gray, or black are good standbys.
- » Shoes—Black or brown dress shoes for men. More flexibility for women with focus on coordination with the color and style of the outfit.
- » Accessories—Noticeable but not overbearing.
- » Tie clip—Optional based on your style comfort and only works with thinner ties.
- » Handbag—coordinated with outfit; same is true for computer bag if a laptop is needed for the meeting. Make the bag complement your style.

Shop it out or pull things from other people's drawers

This is perhaps the most fun, frustrating, and expensive action: go shopping. Again, make sure you feel like you can conquer the world as your authentic self in whatever you put together.

OR

Borrow an outfit, or pieces of an outfit. You are not alone if you don't have the money to shop. But you have friends, and they perhaps can loan you the right things. [Side note: I have a fashion-industry friend who has written about how to dress upscale by shopping at Goodwill, Salvation Army, and other outlet stores. You would be amazed at the high-quality things that people donate to thrift shops.)

Update your résumé—spend time up-leveling your work descriptions

Take the time to update your résumé and ensure it accurately captures your:

- » Freshman on-campus job (if applicable)
- » Summer job between your freshman and sophomore year (if applicable)
- » Job title—update to target summer internship jobs
- » Job profile—ensure this accurately captures your present profile and strengths
- » Freshman activities, awards, skills, and leadership

Spruce up your work experience bullets

I provided some basic examples of how to flesh out a cashier and babysitter job into a bit of illustrative detail. Now, I want to dig deeper into how to think about the bullets you put under your various positions. I have three concepts for you—parallel language, action verbs with impact, and priority. I'll bring these concepts to life using bullets pulled straight from a résumé I was recently reviewing (disguised to protect the innocent). Here is the original job work description.

Logistics Executive Team Manager

» Re-designed warehouse layout to enable DISGUISED.com growth of 220% within three months

» Store replenishment payroll decreased by 26% while overall sales increased 7%

» Responsible for distribution management for DISGUISED in-store, e-commerce and Google Express

» Number one backroom location accuracy in the Northwest Region (56 other locations)

» Selected to pilot Google Express and DISGUISED integration - maintained 99.2% fill rate and 100% packed on time

» Plan and executed seasonal transitions as well as new product launches

» Lead technology insertion

» Directly managed six teams totaling 40 employees, including four team leads

#1 Ensure content is parallel

Your bullets should be parallel with each other. They should all be the same tense. They should all be the same type of things—like are they an impact you made, a responsibility you had, or a combination of both? Let's dissect the above to illustrate the differences in these eight bullets.

Past tense, impact
» Store replenishment payroll decreased by 26% while overall sales increased 7%
» Selected to pilot Google Express and DISGUISED integration - maintained 99.2% fill rate and 100% packed on time

Past tense, responsibility
» Directly managed six teams totaling 40 employees, including four team leads

Past tense, responsibility and impact
» Re-designed warehouse layout to enable DISGUISED.com growth of 220% within three months

Current tense, responsibility
» Responsible for distribution management for DISGUISED in-store, e-commerce and Google Express
» Lead technology insertion

Current tense, impact

» Number one backroom location accuracy in the Northwest Region (56 other locations)

Both current and past tense, responsibility

» Plan and executed seasonal transitions as well as new product launches

That's a lot of variety. Your current jobs should be described in current tense. Your past jobs should be described in past tense.

#2 Combine action verbs with impact

Bullets should use a variety of powerful action verbs. Action verbs are specific, clarify your contributions, and bring a confident tone to your résumé. Ensure you don't use the same one twice. Use online searches to get ideas like launched, managed, maintained, increased, developed, evaluated, executed, analyzed, motivated—you get the gist.

Whenever you can, combine your action verbs with quantifiable results. For example:

» Increased social media followers by 15% through execution of new social media approach
» Created marketing collateral for a new product launch which exceeded sales targets by 23%
» Delivered 10x more sales leads through creative approach to email subject lines

#3 Priority

Now, let's talk about priority. There is a famous Mark Twain quote, "I didn't have time to write a short letter, so I wrote a long one instead." Editing takes work. You need to do that editing work on your résumé. If you give me a laundry list of bullets, you give me nothing but noise. I tune out to all of it. Don't make me have to concentrate to read. I'd say, shortlist no more than four or five. How do you pick? Without having a specific job in mind that you are applying for, think about the ones that most illustrate things like taking initiative, problem-solving, communication, and delivering results. When you do have a specific job in mind, update to the most job-relevant bullets for that job.

Let's bring it all together. I took a shot at updating the original résumé bullets to reflect my guidance. Before that, I added a short description of the overall responsibilities of the position to set context. Note the bullets are all past tense, start with an action verb, include impact, and illustrate select skills used to achieve the impact (for example, leading, being proactive, and collaborating)

Logistics Executive Team Manager
Managed all distribution across in-store, e-commerce, and Google Express.

» Earned #1 backroom location accuracy leading a team of 40 (out of 56 other locations)

» Enabled 220 percent sales growth through proactive redesign of warehouse layout

» Maintained 99.2 percent fill rate and 100 percent on-time packing collaborating on Google Express pilot

Reads better, right? Use consistent tense and language. Use strong illustrative action verbs (for example, earned, enabled, leading, proactive). Prioritize bullets.

Think about where you want to step up to grow further

We had a bit of a deep dive on your bullets. Now step back and check out your current résumé. How does it look? Are there areas where your gut tells you that you need more? I encourage you to explore a new activity or club to add to your interests. This is great for your résumé but is also part of continuing the college experience to learn about yourself, have fun, and expand your network. Also, where can you step up and take on a leadership position?

Keep building out your résumé

This one is very straightforward—refresh your résumé.

» Update your résumé with new content.
» Spruce up your work experience bullets— parallel, impactful, and prioritized.
» Proofread it.

Set up LinkedIn—the front door to employers and your lifelong network

With your updated résumé, you are now ready to create your LinkedIn profile. This will become your front door to prospective employers and a critical tool for networking throughout your career.

In addition to your résumé, you will also need two other things—a headshot and a cover photo. When you sign up, be sure to use an email that you are, or can be, in the habit of checking at least every day. As contacts and recruiters interact with you on LinkedIn, you will receive email alerts and want to respond in a timely manner.

Headshot

This is straightforward, but it is surprising how many people get it wrong. Once you sign up, you can click on "My Network" and scan the photos of others. This should give you an idea of what works and what doesn't. Essentially, you need a smiling, close-up photo of yourself groomed and wearing something professional. That's it. Here are some tips.

> ### Do
> » Ensure you are smiling with your eyes as well as your teeth. You want to convey warmth and energy.
> » Have your face in focus with a background that

is somewhat blurry and doesn't take away from
your smiling face.

» Crop the photo so your head takes up about
2/3 of the top of the photo with your neck and
shoulders in the bottom third—there should be
some border around your hair and face.

Do Not

» Have others in the photo—people or animals

» Use a photo where you look drunk, unfriendly,
or goofy.

» Look off outside the picture in some weird way.

» Use a full body shot where people can't see
your face.

» Crop your face too closely so it looks huge
relative to others online.

Cover photo

There are a few different options that work for
young professional cover photos. Once you are employed,
your employer may have a branded template for you to
use. Until then, here are three options. You'll need some
trial and error in terms of cropping the photos to work
in the frame.

» *College background*—Get images of your college
and find a good horizontal one that you think
is Instagram worthy. I especially recommend
this option if you are at a top university. As you

communicate and network with alumni, they may be more drawn to assist when they see your passion for your school.

» *City background*—Get images of your city and find a good horizontal one.

» *Use the default*—I see a lot of people just using a default template and that is totally fine.

Once you have your two photos, you can then upload them and fill your résumé content into your profile. The interface is straightforward. Be sure to have someone else proofread for any spelling errors. Seriously, don't skip someone else proofreading.

Final note, from your profile you can note a status near the top. Set yours up so it reads "open to opportunities." You'll want this status until you land that first job after graduation.

Seems pretty legit right? This is a major step in the adulting process.

Start building your network

The final step is to start building out your network. I would encourage you to connect only to those people you would feel comfortable reaching out to and engaging on a topic or asking for help in some way. It is also important that connections would say positive things about you. Think about a prospective employer reaching out and asking any of these connections about you— you would want them to be an advocate. You should not connect to everyone you have ever met. Go to "My Network" and start hitting the "Connect" button.

Here are some starter ideas:

» Your parents and other family
» Your parent's friends that you know well
» Previous managers and co-workers
» Professors you have built relationships with so far
» Club advisors
» Greek life advisors and alums
» College friends and upperclassmen
» High school friends

In this first pass, try to connect to at least twenty-five people. As those people accept your connections, the algorithm will get smarter and, each time you visit the "My Network" page, the names that come up will more likely be people you know.

For close contacts, you can just hit "Connect." For others where the relationship is more distant, it is worth adding a note. I personally am more likely to accept new requests if there is short note. Here is a general one you can use as a base.

> John,
> 	*I'm starting to build out my network and would love to be connected. Thank you!*
> 	*Best,*
> 	*Brian*

I encourage you to personalize it to each person where possible. Here is the same base note but with one sentence of personalization as to why I want to connect to this person. Where possible, add a sentence like that.

> *John,*
>> *I'm starting to build out my network and would love to be connected. I've always appreciated your great advice. Thank you!*
>> *Best,*
>> *Brian*

Set up your front door

Set up your LinkedIn and target to get to your first fifty connections in a couple weeks. Revisit once a month, or so, and spend time reviewing potential new connections to add—striving to get a few hundred by the end of the school year.

Set up Handshake—an excellent welcome mat to finding a first job

If LinkedIn is your front door to the whole professional world, Handshake (joinhandshake) is your most excellent welcome mat to that front door. Handshake is only for connecting employers with entry-level post college jobs to students in school—you need an .edu email just to sign up. Thousands of employers use Handshake and hundreds of universities partner with them. Hit the big sign-up button and follow the steps. Use that same friendly-faced photo we just talked about. If your university doesn't use Handshake, find out if they use one of the similar offerings and sign up for that.

Once signed up, spend a bit of time exploring around and getting familiar. Learn how the search tool works to find jobs, as well as check out the topic areas they have under Career Tips. If you know what's there, you may remember to go back and read when you need it.

Work on landing a summer internship—use holiday and spring breaks to network

Now that we have some basics in place, there is one last action for your sophomore year—work on landing a summer internship. I am purposeful in my language to work at it, and it's okay if you don't actually land an internship this coming summer. Landing an internship in the area of your major is more important the summer after your junior year. Just by working at it, you will be building your muscles around email communications and conversation. You'll be ahead of the game when it comes to next summer and when you are working on your full-time position search.

Much of the work happens about a month before your breaks—I'm only asking for three hours (twice)

I know you have a lot going on—and, when you don't, you're probably getting some much-needed sleep.

Adding on a job search may seem like too much. So, I want you to start with just a three-hour block of time in early November on a day when your classes are light. Put it on your planner.

Before diving into what you will do in that three-hour time block, let's talk about digital communities and job boards beyond LinkedIn and Handshake. There are many, and new ones come along all the time. Indeed, Monster, and ZipRecruiter are three of the broadly popular ones. Beyond the broadly focused sites, there are also niche sites for specific industries. For example: MediaBistro (media and creative), Jobs.art (the arts), Careers.Broadway (links to a number of early-career theatre job sites), Dice (technology), IHireBiotechnology (biology, chemical, and pharma), Space-Careers (space and defense), USAJobs.gov (federal government jobs), Governmentjobs (local government), Nexxt (targeted industries like Construction, Healthcare, Hospitality, Entertainment, and more). To find others related to your target field, simply search "Find a job in INSERT" and see what you discover.

Back to your three-hour time block, here is what you are going to do:

1. Go visit your friend at the Career Center. Tell them you are working on landing a summer internship and want to make the most of your holiday break. Ask if they have any advice or recommendations. Follow their advice.

2. Sit down, fire up your laptop, and put your phone on airplane mode (if you don't put it on airplane mode then please make it a five-hour block to account for the distractions).

3. Go to LinkedIn, Handshake, and a few from the plethora of other sites and search for internships—try different modifiers like "marketing intern" etc. Find five that seem interesting. More if you're feeling it.

4. Search whether you have any connections at those companies.

5. Reach out to your connections and ask if they know anything about the role and would be willing to help get your résumé to the right person related to the internship (include the link) and act accordingly based on their responses. Ideally you could meet up in person, or interview, over your upcoming break.

6. Feel free to apply online. Typically, the odds are lower on this approach, but it doesn't hurt to try. There are some tips on the logistics for applying in the junior year if you feel ambitious and want to apply those tips this year. No guilt if you don't.

If on a roll, try five more. You get the idea. Repeat these same steps about a month before spring break— again timed so you could meet up in person and/or interview over the break. That's all I suggest for this first attempt. Just know that you're building your professional muscles. I'll go into more detail about how to network and leverage your contacts in the Junior year section. That will then feed into a more rigorous attempt to land an internship for the summer after your junior year.

If you land an internship, awesome. Congrats! Make the most of it! I suggest you jump ahead and read the Final Thoughts section at the end of this book which has some general advice on how to show up to a job, and life for that matter. In case it is not obvious, if you excel at a summer internship, chances are that employer will want to offer you a full-time role upon your graduation. Over your summer, try to meet with as many people as you can. Set yourself a weekly target. Don't forget to connect to people on LinkedIn to grow your network.

Give it a shot to land a summer internship

Commit six hours—2 three-hour blocks in November and the Spring—that's not that bad. I know you can find six hours in the school year. Put in the work. If you succeed and land an internship, that's great. If you don't, know that by going through these motions, you built up your professional muscles. Remember to check your email at least daily once you have communications out to working professionals—letting days go by is not cool.

Sophomore recap

How did it go? I hope you accomplished a good number of actions. Remember, even if you didn't land a summer internship, all these things are moving you forward and leading you to being in a stronger position when you are interviewing for full-time positions your senior year. Oh, and hey, are you continuing to build relationships with your professors and advisor? Remember we covered that freshman year.

Heart: Homing in

- » Committed to investing in myself and taking the adulting actions.
- » Aggressively pondered my major (bonus points for landing on it).

Social: Adulting your communications

- » Like, killed my use of filler words. I mean, uh, like, I did.
- » Started practicing professional email communications.
- » Learned conversation basics—preparation, curiosity, and follow up.
- » Attended my first career fair and talked to four to five target companies.

Career: Looking the part

» Landed a part-time job and am staying conscious of what I like and don't like.

» Acquired an outfit I can conquer the world wearing.

» Updated my resume—joined another new activity and/or landed a leadership role.

» Set up my LinkedIn and connected to at least fifty people.

» Set up my Handshake and explored the resources available.

» Put in the time and worked on landing a summer internship.

Please set a reminder to crack open *A Well-Baked Pie* about a month out from heading back to school.

JUNIOR YEAR

Commit, focus, and really get to know yourself

You are now officially an upperclassman. This is your year to thrive. Before we go there, though, take a moment to revisit your sophomore recap. Are you feeling good about what you accomplished? Feel free to spend a bit of extra time if there are any actions you think need some attention. If not, let's move forward. Just so you know, next Fall you will have both the stress of your academic studies and finding a full-time job. So, enjoy your junior year. It is an amazing one. You're established, you've gone through your college learning curve, and you've either landed on your major, or hopefully you're extremely close.

You'll see that your actions this year build on those from the previous two years. You should be growing into your confidence around where you are headed and how you will get there.

Heart: Finding your story

Related to heart, we've got two repeat topics, and a new one. The new topic will help you dive deep to understand your brand. I'm excited for what you will learn about yourself.

> **Get your shit together reminder #2—only applies if skipped sophomore year**

Did you get your shit together already? If so, that's perfect. If not, seriously, you need to do it now. I meant it when I said it for your sophomore year. It is your life we're talking about. It is also about making the most of your college years. They will be over before you know it.

Check yourself

Yes, invest in yourself. As a reminder, here is a sample of items that reflect whether you have your shit together.

» Studying and going to class
» Being curious about majors and the typical jobs that align to majors
» Getting work experience—for life skills and your résumé

» Trying new activities and getting
leadership positions
» Meeting new people and growing your network
» Morphing from a young adult to a
young professional
» Being active and exercising

Stop pondering your major—accept it and fire up your passion about it

You could, of course, ponder whether you have the right major for all four years of college—probably five or six years if you are pondering and then switching all the time. I'm a fan of the four-year plan. College is expensive, so why add on extra cost? I encouraged exploration freshman year—obsessively curious. I encouraged you to pick something early in your sophomore year—aggressively ponder. Now that you are a junior, I encourage you to accept and fire up your passion about your current major.

Accept and get passionate about what you're learning

What does "accept and fire up passion" mean? By accept and fire up passion, I mean get excited about what you are learning and the potential first jobs you are going to pursue. Stop wasting brain cycles on wondering and worrying if you are on the right path. Just pick the path and go with it. I mentioned at the beginning of this book, your first job or career path will likely not be your last. At this point, you want to increase your odds of landing a great first job, and passion will help you do that.

Passion helps you show up with more confidence

And why does being passionate matter? It matters for a couple of reasons. It changes how you show up and it changes how others respond to you. If you are unsure of your direction, that uncertainty will come through to others—even if you have told yourself to fake being passionate in a conversation. Make the passion real. You picked this major for a reason. Even if you have some nagging doubts, focus on the things you are sure about.

Passion gets others excited about you

As you network, if you are still pondering your major as a junior, people are not going to be impressed. I personally would wonder what you had been doing in college so far. I also wouldn't be as motivated to help connect you to others if I think you are a bit unsure whether you are truly interested in a certain job, organization, discipline, or industry. If you express passion and surety on where you are headed, I will be more inclined to help as I will want to help you fulfill that passion. Others work in a similar fashion.

The only time I recommend switching at this point is if you absolutely hate your major. Even then, talk to your advisor about all the potential job and career options that you could take with your current major before switching. Also, know the cost and time implications of any changes at this point.

Land the plane

Accept what you have picked and get excited about learning. Stop wasting brain cycles on thinking about other majors. Being excited and really thinking of yourself heading down a career path will help you be more connected to the content of your classes. Sincere passion will also help you connect in your conversations at career fairs, networking, and in interviews. Land the plane.

> **Start to define and articulate your brand—what makes you special?**

This one is fun. It is a little off the beaten path, but I think you will enjoy it and get a lot out of it in terms of knowing yourself—and then being able to apply that knowledge to your growth. It is my favorite assignment that I give the Strategic Brand Management class that I teach—and the most impactful for the students. It is all about getting to understand your personal brand.

Let's start with some definitions.

> » *Brand identity* is defined as the set of (aspirational) associations that a company has of its brand.

> » *Brand image* is defined as the set of (actual) associations consumers have with the brand.

We are going to dig into your personal brand identity (what you aspire to be) and your personal brand image (how you are perceived). Understanding how your brand is perceived is critical to build and manage a strong personal brand. The exercise will allow you to understand the gap between your brand identity and your brand image. Here is a simplified version of the assignment that I give to my class.

Assess your personal brand identity (your aspirational traits)

Think about:

> » What are the first five positive words that you associate with yourself?
> » What are three positive traits where you are not strong? (for example, patient is one of mine)

Assess your personal brand image (your actual/perceived traits)

Ask at least ten people (for example, ask friends, family, classmates, colleagues) the following questions. You can ask directly or set up a short SurveyMonkey and have them complete.

> » What are the first five words that come to mind when they think of you?

» What are three positive traits they would not use to describe you? I want to emphasize that they should identify positive traits that you don't have, not negative traits. (For example, patience is a positive trait that others would not use to describe me.)

Create two different word clouds based on the feedback from others

The internet has free software to create word clouds. Input the words:

#1 cloud: Words used to describe you.
#2 cloud: Words noted as the positive traits others would not use to describe you.

Analyze what you have

You should have your self-identified brand identity traits, a word cloud on how others describe you, and another word cloud on the positive traits others would not use to describe you)

» Are there discrepancies between your *brand identity* and *brand image*?
» If so, are there some discrepancies where you would like to close the gap? If so, what are the steps you can take?
» Are there some strengths in your *brand image* that you perhaps weren't aware before?

» Does your *brand image* give you a solid platform to perhaps infuse some attributes into your résumé and into interview conversations?

» Are there positive traits that people would not attribute to you that you would like to develop, or think are important to potential employers?

Write down any actions your analysis inspires

My actual assignment then goes into detail on how to create a brand positioning statement. For our purposes, I think it is enough for you to understand your current brand image and identify areas where you want to move the needle and grow.

Be curious about yourself

Do the personal brand exercise. You are at college to learn and grow right? I assure you this will help you do that in a big way. I'm hoping by reading about the exercise that your curiosity has been fired up to dig in and find out about your personal brand image.

Social: Digging into skills

Your social skills are building so let's keep adding on. I'll start with additional commentary on study abroad and career fairs. I'll hit on leadership. Then we'll cover a personal hot button—punctuality. Punctuality will be a key trait to apply against the big new topic, how to make the most of networking.

Push your social skills—through new experiences and leadership

First of all, it's critical to push your social skills through new experiences and leadership. I'll emphasize growing your social skills for the sake of maturing how you show up, but also gathering more fodder to strengthen your résumé.

Study abroad and experience it all out—and grow and grow and grow

If it's financially viable for you to study abroad, I hope that you do and make the most of the amazing life experience that it is—typically in your junior year, but not always. Study, sure. Also travel, visit museums, immerse in the culture, eat incredible food, and experience it all. When I was in London, one weekend I chose to skip traveling to Dublin to see the band U2 because I had a lot of studying. I still regret that choice. I should have gone. Go. Do. Eat. Drink the beverage of your choice (of course, only according to local drinking age). Be merry.

An international experience should feed your abilities to interact with others, hold great conversations, and show up curious and enthusiastic to life (and job interviews). Wake up curious. Think about the differences in how people live and work. Try new things. Consider how to adapt how you show up in this new culture. Ponder how your views change about people and the world.

Step up into leadership

Freshman year I encouraged getting involved. That's just the start. If you haven't already, these next two years, step up into leadership roles. That's what employers want to see. If you are in the Greek system, there are all kinds of leadership opportunities. My son was president of his fraternity his junior year and that responsibility grew his social capability in so many ways—interpersonal dynamics, team dynamics, management, leadership, and so much more.

Clubs also need leaders. Whatever you are involved in, figure out how you either step up to an official leadership role, or take on responsibility for an initiative. You will be challenged and grow from it.

Remember to add your international study and any leadership positions to your résumé.

Go. Do. Eat. Drink. Be merry. Oh, and lead people.

Make the most of your experience. If you have the luxury to go abroad, go full out. Come back exhausted and broke. Whether you go abroad or stay, step up your involvement from member to leader—push yourself into new situations and responsibilities.

> **Attack more career fairs—be a bright spot in the day of every recruiter**

If you do study abroad, this may be a conflicting message as you will miss some career opportunities if you are out of the country. That said, if you are around, make the most of what is offered. My advice for career fairs is much the same as that for your sophomore year. The one difference is your objective. Last year your primary objectives were to explore and learn about companies, get ideas for classes to take as preparation, and a little bit to learn about internship opportunities. This time around your objective should be focused on landing a summer internship.

Feel free to go back and reread the detailed recommendations for attending career fairs. The summary version is:

» Prepare—identify your four to five target companies and conduct research
» Groom—show up energetic and polished
» Get there early
» Be strategic by warming up with some companies that are not your targets
» Engage with your targets—introduction, solid handshake, smile, and curiosity
» Get a business card
» Connect on LinkedIn and follow up—concise, clear, passionate, appreciative, and professional

I have one additional recommendation on preparation. Revisit your notes on who you met last year from any of companies that you are going to target again this year. Many times, the same people will be there, and it will be great if you can walk up remembering faces, names, and aspects of your conversation from last time.

Watch for panels, presentations, workshops, and seminars

Beyond the career fair, throughout the year your career center is likely hosting a variety of career-focused panels, presentations, workshops, and seminars. Watch for those and make time to attend. When they are over, move to the front of the room and introduce yourself in similar fashion to your interactions at career fairs. Who knows what will come out of your introduction, but it will be certainly be better than what would come from quietly sneaking out the back door.

Be a bright spot

Strive to be a bright spot in the day of every recruiter you encounter at career fairs. If you can do that, you've nailed it.

Respect others—early is on time

On time is late. Let me say it again. On time is late. If you are meeting me for coffee at 10:30 a.m., do not arrive at 10:30. Arrive at 10 and sit in the parking lot or walk around the block. The practical aspects of this are that being caught in traffic due to weather or an accident will not exacerbate your inherent jitters over the meeting. Come in at 10:10 and get a table. Sit there and get your mind in the right headspace until I arrive at some time between 10:20 and 10:30. You should be there first.

A couple of months ago I was meeting the brother of my daughter's good friend. He is the same age as my son and had reached out to get some career guidance. I was happy to meet up. Both our homes are just a few minutes away from Starbucks. I got there at 10:20. He got there at 10:37. It was Saturday morning and yes, I was keeping track of the time as I had things to do and I was there to help him out. When he arrived, he did not acknowledge or apologize about being late. I hate that. If you are late, which sometimes cannot be helped, be profusely apologetic in the moment as well as in your follow up note. When you are late, you are stealing time from someone. My friend's father, a career Marine, taught her from an early age: "Be fifteen minutes early for everything to make sure you are late for nothing."

In my life I have come to realize there are those that are conscious and respectful of others' time and there are those that are not. If you are known for being late, I highly recommend you adjust your relationship with time. Besides being respectful, being early allows you to get centered and calm before your interactions. When you are running late and rushed you show up more frenetic and sweaty—neither of which is great for meeting new people.

And can I tell you the worst thing you can do? The *very* worst thing you can do is arrive late with a

Starbucks in your hand. If you are ever late and stopped for coffee at some point along the way, throw it out before showing up.

Be early

Early is on time. I mean it. Assume the worst will happen in your travel to meet people and then add in time to account for that. For example, if you know your freeway time can range from twenty minutes on a good day to forty-five on a bad day, then plan for sixty. Getting places early is not a bad thing—you can get centered, think about your questions, and get comfortable with the environment.

> **Learn to network coffee/call—it's a lifelong skill that will serve you well**

It would be truly amazing to get a summer internship just from going to the career fair. Amazing but it rarely happens. It's like the lottery. Somebody wins it. The odds of it being you though are low. So, if you don't get an internship from the career fair, how do you get one? Applying on the internet? Nope. Hoping? Nope. Praying? Nope. The answer is networking. Lots of networking.

You do not get summer internships by applying on the internet—you don't get full time jobs that way either. Like winning the lottery, it is possible, but the odds are low. If you are applying to an internship posting from a company worth working for, the chances are that hundreds of others are too. You are all going into the same big pile or online screener. The chances of somebody seeing your résumé and reaching back out are very small—very small indeed. One mentee that I started working with had submitted her résumé to sixty different job postings. She didn't hear back from one. Applying cold rarely works. That is why you have to network. You need to get on the radar of a person who can help you.

Networking fundamentals—whether over coffee, lunch, videoconference, or call

A networking conversation can happen several ways. They can be in person over coffee or lunch, or virtual via videoconference or call. The main difference for in-person meetings is they have the additional aspect of payment for coffee or lunch. Think of the general flow as:

» Identifying target contact
» Reaching out and scheduling
» Meeting (and paying if in person)
» Following up

Networking conversations can be used for a few different learning reasons. A few of the more common reasons to meet include learning about:

- » A person's industry or role
- » A company
- » An open posted position
- » Advice on classes or majors for a specific career direction
- » The possibility of an internship
- » Another person (for example, somebody who is going to interview you)

The value of your network grows directly with the growth of your contacts

There are many people who can help you with your job search and your LinkedIn first-degree connections will be the foundation of networking throughout your career. Keep systematically building out your network. Let's revisit the initial list we used to build out your LinkedIn connections.

- » Your parents and other family
- » Your parent's friends that you know well
- » Previous managers and co-workers
- » Professors you have built relationships with so far
- » Club advisors
- » Greek life advisors and alums
- » College friends and upperclassmen
- » High school friends

For networking, you can connect with all of these, plus a couple others that will likely push you further beyond your comfort as you reach out and meet with them. The additions include two types of individuals working at either your target companies, or industry competitors of target companies:

> » Alumni from your school
> » Second-degree contacts

Recent alumni working in your target companies can be an especially great resource as they were able to land there, likely have similar pedigree, and may be inclined to help fellow schoolmates with their job search efforts. People working at competitors of your target companies are also great places to fire up conversations to get intelligence about your target companies, the industry, or possibly opportunities at the other companies in the industry. Second degree contacts are generally open to communicating or helping you since you know people in common (your first-degree contacts).

LinkedIn also has something called InMail where you can pay to connect with people outside your network. Start with the free route but consider purchasing InMail if there is a particular company you are interested in working at and don't have any contacts. I know recruiters that like it when someone has researched their company and then take the opportunity to write a thoughtful InMail referencing why they want to work there.

Identifying networking targets

How do you actually identify specific target individuals?

Given the broad scope of LinkedIn, I'll go a litter deeper on the how. The LinkedIn interface is constantly evolving and improving but it all starts with the search. Then, you have three main paths to identify those you'd like to reach. Through all the searches below, you are ideally looking to find first and second degree contacts. Once you get to the screen of potential contacts just scroll through viewing faces and titles—just keep clicking in on people to read more detail until you find those you think might have an interesting perspective to help you.

> » *Schools*—Find your School, click on the Alumni
> » *Companies*—Find your target Company, click on the People
> » *Jobs*—Search for "Internship" or internship with various modifiers, click on the Connections

Similar to the broad array of job board sites, there are also many more options to network based on your area of interest. Joining relevant LinkedIn and Facebook groups is one way people come together around common interests and fields. Also, each industry typically has focused professional groups. For example: ICMA.org (local government), AIAS.org (architecture), HumanResources.org (HR professionals), AAHAM.

org (healthcare administration), and the diversity of options goes on. Ask your professors, your career center friend, and upperclassman where else they are building out their networks for your field of interest and follow their lead.

Reaching out and scheduling—use the basics of conciseness and clarity

Just using LinkedIn as an example, once you are ready to reach out to somebody, you can Message them through LinkedIn if you are a 1st degree contact. If not, you can Connect and add a message to your request. If they are in your same location, I would suggest trying for coffee as an in-person meeting typically results in a stronger relationship. If they are not in your location, aim for a "short call or video." In your message, use the basics we covered on professional email communications—concise, clear, passionate, appreciative, and professional. Here is an example with a 2nd degree contact at a company you see has an open internship position. In the message, you reference your common contact. There are many ways you can position your message— this is just one example.

> *Mark,*
>
> *I'm a friend of NAME. I'm ABC University class of 202X and working to land an internship at COMPANY. Do you have 30 minutes for me to buy you a coffee? I am interested in asking you*

*questions about COMPANY and perhaps learn
about open internship roles. Are there some options
that work the week of X/X? I am very happy to
come to you if that works best.*

*I really appreciate you considering this.
Thank you so much!*
    Best,
    Brian

Sometimes they may not have time to meet with you. Another potential positive outcome is, just by expressing that you are working hard to land an internship, they may offer to help get you to the right person. Being forwarded to the right person has much more potential to result in an interview than applying cold.

The meeting—some finer points of polish

I've already covered how to show up well in conversation, so I won't belabor that here. If your meeting is over coffee or lunch, I want to emphasize that you should offer to pay. And you should be fairly emphatic about paying since they are spending their time to help you. Many will insist they pay because you are in college, and they are working. It is fine if they end up paying if you truly pushed on it a couple times. If they do pay, express your gratitude.

Even though these may not be formal interviews, you should still dress professionally. Remember, everything is in some way an interview.

Beyond the questions you ask about the topic you are learning about, one additional powerful question to ask near the end of a networking conversation is:

"Are there any other people that come to mind that you think would be good for me to speak with?"

Follow up—yes, follow up

Nothing new here. Always follow up expressing gratitude and clarifying any next steps.

Get caffeinated

Identify a target contact or two, reach out, and set up a networking coffee or call/video. Pick one of the following learning areas:

- » A person's industry or role
- » A company
- » An open posted position
- » Advice on classes or majors for a specific career direction
- » The possibility of an internship
- » Another person (for example, somebody who is going to interview you)

The more you do these, the more comfortable you will become.

> **Know the nuances for video interactions— background grunge is not cool**

While I think the in-person coffees are your best bet to make positive impressions and form relationships, I realize you may not be located in the same city as networking contacts and video certainly has become much more the norm in the last couple of years. Let's cover a few easy things to ensure you come off in the most positive way when video is involved.

Download and test any software you need well before the actual video call

There is nothing worse than being late from technical difficulties that could have easily been avoided. You don't want to be watching your software download three minutes after your meeting was supposed to start.

Think about what the other person will see

Ensure your face is well lit and you don't have a bright window, or light, hitting you from the side or from behind causing a dark shadow on your whole face or half of it. Wear professional attire above the waist. Most importantly, think about your background and environment. Does it look clean? Organized? Professional? Avoid background noise by turning off your mobile phone and asking your dog to take a nap. Avoid interruption by telling others in your household what you are doing. Consider booking a room at the library if your home turf isn't a good option. Also, most platforms allow you to blur your background if you can't quite get it looking polished behind you.

Prep your materials

Print out your résumé and the highlighted job description. Create notes on the top three to four points you want to ensure you cover. Noodle on the stories you will tell to illustrate how you align well to what's important on the job description (more on storytelling later). Have a few questions ready.

Look at the camera

If you are on a laptop and looking at the other person's face, you aren't making eye contact—you are looking down, up, or sideways. Look at the camera and periodically glance at their face on the screen. Final thought, once you're rolling, smile, breathe, and be present in your conversation.

About twenty years ago, I learned about looking at the camera the hard way. A recruiter had screened me over video, liked me, but had to then encourage me to have better eye contact in my next round of interviews. It was in our feedback conversation that I realized I had looked at her face on the screen rather than at the camera above the screen. It was a great lesson that has stuck with me. I did end up getting that position, so it all ended well.

Get ready for lights, camera, action

Make the most of video interactions. Be ready with the software. Think about the full experience from the other person's perspective—your face and your environment. Finally, look at the camera.

Career: Landing an internship

Let's wrap up your junior year with some advice around the logistics of the application process, and then apply those tips as you tackle landing a summer internship for this final summer of college.

Raise your application game—six habitual steps for applying

I've said the strongest path to landing a job is through networking. You need to actually apply though. I've got six steps to run through each time you are applying. Before that, I have a one-time action.

Clean up your social media

What impression would a recruiter get if they dug into your Instagram feed and started scrolling? What about your Twitter feed? What about your Facebook timeline if you are old school and have one? If you are confident in how you have shown up online over the years, don't sweat it too much. Your online profile might be consistent and reinforcing of the best qualities you are putting forth on your résumé, LinkedIn, Handshake, and in interviews.

If you aren't confident, check your privacy settings and reduce access to only friends where possible. I encourage to go a step further and take down anything that might be questionable to a future employer. By questionable, I mean anything where you could be considered irresponsible, narcissistic, entitled, unkind, lazy, and I'm sure there are some other things I am forgetting. You get the idea.

Six habitual steps to consider every time you apply

With your social media all buttoned up, here are the six steps I recommend every time you apply for something. It sounds like a lot but once you build the habit it won't take much time.

1. **Print and highlight the job description.**
   Highlight the key things they are looking for in candidates. As you highlight, be thinking about those that most resonate for what you bring.

2. **Check if you meet roughly 50-75 percent or more of the requirements.** There are studies and articles that men will look at a list of job requirements and, if they meet a good number of them, will apply. Women will look at the same list, meet the same number of requirements or more, and not apply because they don't feel they meet the criteria. Regardless of the validity of the studies and the reasons behind the behavioral difference, my advice is to think you fit the requirements. It doesn't hurt to try. Consider the job description the company's wish list.

3. **Customize your résumé.** Take your highlighted job description and use it to do a few things

to your résumé. If you have a target title or position at the top, match what they call the role. Now, look at the highlighted job description and infuse some of those same words and traits into the three to four sentences you have at the top in your professional profile section.

4. **Consider a short cover letter.** I've worked in technology for a long time. Cover letters aren't much of a thing in the technology industry. If you are applying into more conservative industries like insurance or say, oil and gas, you might consider creating a short cover letter. You have to think about how staid your target industry is and adjust accordingly on whether to include a cover letter or not. If you're unsure, ask your friend in the career center on their thoughts. If you include one, grab their attention on how you are a strong culture fit and can bring it on the required skills. Don't reiterate your résumé—highlight a few key points and remember these guidelines: concise, clear, passionate, appreciative, and professional.

5. **Be thorough and accurate in your application.** Don't do stuff like put today's date in the birthday field. Don't misspell things. Punctuate. Use proper grammar. Proofread.

6. Attempt to connect to a recruiter and express interest. Finally, get back on LinkedIn or other networking sites and see if you can find a recruiter to connect to at the company. If it is a large company, it may be impossible to get to the recruiter working on the specific role—that's okay. Others can try to get you into the right recruiter or hiring manager hands.

If you are looking to get into local or federal government, the process will vary by local government and you should visit the site of the city, county, or state. For federal jobs, usajobs.gov has very clear instructions on how to register and search.

Increase your odds

Put in the time with every application. Ensure your social media reflects the you that you have become and want to show the professional world. Then, each time you apply, be disciplined to follow the six steps.

1. Print and highlight the job description

2. Check if you meet 50% or more of the requirements

3. Customize your résumé

4. Consider a short cover letter

5. Be thorough and accurate in your application

6. Attempt to connect to a recruiter and express interest

Strive to land a summer internship— this summer it's more important

A summer internship this year can pave the way to your full-time role. Last year I said it is okay to not land a summer internship—but you needed to try. Rather than try, I've switched up the verb to strive. Strive to land a summer internship—and attack the search with more grit and perseverance. We've built on your networking skills, so this year there is a little more work. Once again, update your résumé to get it current—do the same for LinkedIn and Handshake when you're done. Now, start the search.

1. Go visit your friend at the Career Center— you should be major buds by now. Tell them you are again working on landing a summer internship. Ask if they have any advice or recommendations. Follow their advice.

2. Sit down, fire up your laptop and put your phone on airplane mode (remember to double or triple the time if you don't use airplane mode).

3. Go to LinkedIn, Handshake, and two or three others search for internships—try different modifiers like "marketing intern" etc. Find five that seem interesting. More if you're feeling it.

4. NEW: Identify five target companies where you would love to work over the summer but

maybe you don't see any open intern positions. These could be companies you know are good employers in your home city/town.

5. Search whether you have any connections at the ten companies now on your list.

6. Reach out to your connections and communicate your desire to land an internship and act accordingly based on their responses.

7. Feel free to apply online. Also, cross your fingers.

During your sophomore year, I suggested time boxing your research and networking effort to three hours the month before the holiday break and another three hours the month before spring break. This time three hours might just be your start. Put in the three hours. Then try to find ten more companies. Put in the time on those. Then try some more. The more you play, the more chances to win—like the lottery. Apply your grit and perseverance.

Attack your internship search

Strive to land an internship. Put in the work. Then put in some more work. Then use your grit and put in some more work. This is all great at building your preparation, networking, and perseverance muscles. If you put in the work and still don't get an internship, that's okay. You put in a valiant effort and that is all anyone can ask.

Junior recap

Hopefully you feel these actions building on the foundation you created your freshman and sophomore years. Keep growing. Keep working to become that well-baked pie that employers will fight over.

Heart: Finding your story

» Got my shit fully together—and never want to hear this reminder again.
» Fully accepted my major and fired up my passion.
» Explored my brand image and put actions in place where I saw improvement areas.

Social: Digging into skills

» Went all out making the most of my international experience (if applicable).
» Made the most out of career fairs and furthered some professional relationships.
» Adopted "early" as my new "on time" and started enjoying the time to get settled.
» Practiced networking coffee/call (s) and grew my comfort level.
» Thought through how to bring my A game to video calls.

Career: Landing an internship

» Stepped up my application smarts—all starting with the job description.
» Applied some serious grit to land a summer internship.

Set a reminder to spend time with *A Well-Baked Pie* about a month out from heading back to school.

SENIOR YEAR

This is it.
Nine months to the real world

Home stretch. Time flies. Let's keep building.

Heart: Getting reflective

I'm going to assume you have landed on a major and have a good pulse on the entry level roles available to that major. I have only one final thing in the heart category. It isn't so much career advice, as it is life advice. It is about taking a moment to be introspective.

> Take a moment—how you will make the most of your final year?

Pause. Ponder. Think about the close friends you have now that three years ago you didn't even know.

Think about some of your highs. Your accomplishments. Your lows. The things you have overcome and conquered. Think about any regrets. I mean it, think about these things. Go somewhere quiet, get out a piece of paper, and write down the following headers with room to write. Then fill it in. Don't over think it. What comes to mind about your last three years? Think back to your starting point of arriving on campus and walking into your dorm room for the first time and contrast it to where you are now.

> » I accomplished:
> » I conquered:
> » I appreciate:
> » I'm most proud of:
> » I regret:

Spend some time wallowing in your accomplishments and appreciation. Many times, we go too quickly by the good things to focus on areas to improve. Don't do that. Wallow for a minute in the goodness.

Are you wallowing? Okay let's take all that and now revisit the seven ingredients for a well-rounded candidate and answer two more questions on your sheet of paper:

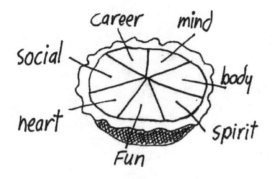

» Of the seven ingredients, the ones I spent the most effort on are:
» The ones I spent the least effort on are:

I have a couple final questions which you can consider in context of your introspection and other answers.

» In my senior year, I want to spend more time:
» In my senior year, I commit to further growing myself by:

Hopefully that was a fun and insightful exercise and leaves you thinking more intentionally about your senior year and these final months before the working world (or grad school). As a quick aside, if you are planning to get an MBA or do further graduate studies, I generally recommend you work for at least several years first. It just makes sense to get some deeper job and life experience before making that additional investment.

Stop and Pause

Pause. Get quiet. Think. Really think. Grab some paper and answer these questions for yourself. You only get one senior year so live it wisely. Attack it with gusto.

» I accomplished:
» I conquered:
» I appreciate:
» I'm most proud of:
» I regret:
» Of the seven ingredients, the ones I spent the most effort on are:
» The ones I spent the least effort on are:
» In my senior year, I want to spend more time:
» In my senior year, I commit to further growing myself by:

Social: Becoming a storyteller

It is time for the polish. It is time for some final baking of your pie. We've covered a lot so far:

» Handshake
» Eye contact
» Speaking volume
» Filler words
» Conversation
» Professional communications

We have one very important skill to talk about, and then another moment of introspection to do some more positive wallowing as well as get real on any areas that still need work.

Learn to tell pithy and compelling stories—it separates you from the pack

"If history were taught in the form of stories, it would never be forgotten." Rudyard, Kipling

If preparation, curiosity, and follow up are Conversation 101, think of storytelling as Conversation 201 or maybe even Conversation 301. This is about learning to be a storyteller. When you are asked about your strongest traits, you should not merely answer with the traits. You need a story to show the traits in action. When you are asked about a previous job, you need a story to bring it to life in a way that is relevant to the job you are trying to land. When you are asked about why you should be chosen for the job, you need a story that resonates. Bottom line: you need to get good at telling stories—not just now, but throughout your life. You may have picked up that I like frameworks. Here is one for storytelling.

- » Consider your audience needs
- » Decide on a compelling headline
- » Build out the story with a start, middle, and end
- » Right-size the detail to bring it to life
- » Tell your story with energy

#1 Consider your audience needs—what are they looking for?

Let's start with two acronyms:

» WIIFM
» WSIC

Any guesses? Well:

» WIIFM: What's in it for me?
» WSIC: Why should I care?

As you choose what story to tell in any given situation, think about what's in it for the other person and why they should care about what you're sharing. What experience or anecdote is most relevant as a starting place to illustrate the point or points you are trying to communicate to the other person?

#2 Decide on a compelling headline—what's the key thing you are trying to get across?

Let's assume a lot of your professional interactions are now going to be interviews. In that case, you are most likely using stories to bring your positive traits to life. You may want to revisit the branding exercise you did to see if you think about your brand identity and image any differently now that more time has gone by. In your stories, you will be trying to convey traits like attention to detail, leadership, work ethic, drive, ability to collaborate, ability to problem-solve, passion, and the list goes on. Pick a headline for your story. Here are some examples of what I mean by the headline of a story—it is your main point.

> » I'm detailed-oriented and love numbers.
> » I'm incredibly strong at problem solving.
> » People love working with me.
> » I'm relentless in achieving my goals.

#3 Build out the story with a start, middle, and end—do you have an arc to the story?

You need to bring your headline to life through a story that shows and proves it. A good story needs structure. Think about movies. They start by setting context on characters and setting, actions happen with the drama building to a climax, and then it ends with some final resolution. Let's use a similar framework for building your stories:

> » *Start*—start with a pithy version of your headline message and then provide context for the story (for example, who, what, when)
> » *Middle*—illustrate the actions taken and any challenges
> » *End*—communicate the story resolution

#4 Right-size the detail to bring it to life—does the detail support your headline?

When talking about writing professional emails, I mentioned the need to be concise and clear. No reason we can't apply those adjectives again here for stories. Concise and clear is great but stories also need detail to bring them to life in a meaningful and visual way. What do I mean by right-size the detail? I mean, figure out the right points of detail that paint a picture, but don't go overboard in detail and don't meander. I'll show an example of what I mean in a moment.

#5 Tell your story with energy—are you telling it with some vocal variety and enthusiasm?

Think of your most boring professor. Got them in mind? Now think of your most engaging and entertaining professor. Got them in mind? Now, think about the difference in how each showed up in the classroom. I'm going to guess the engaging and entertaining professor showed up with passion, smiled a lot, exuded energy, and used vocal variety that mixed things up a bit to keep your attention. When telling your story, you want to think about your most engaging and entertaining teacher—and then adopt some of their traits as you tell your stories.

You must read the non-verbal signals of those to whom you are telling your story. Do they seem engaged? Or bored? Does it look like they are tracking with your story or getting lost as you meander through a myriad of detail that is taking away from your main story thread. I want to emphasize you can always ask somebody if they want more detail if you aren't sure you have given them enough. That is a better option than talking too much and leaving them with the impression that you aren't a great communicator.

Let me make up a story to illustrate the first four of the steps

In this scenario, let's pretend a recruiter has just asked you, "What was your favorite class in school?" Let's also pretend your answer is psychology. If you weren't telling a story, you might just answer "psychology" and stare back. That would suck as an answer. Let's go through the steps and I'll make up some things to create a story for illustration purposes.

Consider your audience

» What do you think they hope to learn from asking about your favorite class? One likely option is to understand what fuels your passion and a little bit about the skills you may have acquired in school.

Decide on a headline

» How about, "I love learning about what drives people."

Build out the story

» **Start:** I love learning what drives people. Three classes jump to mind—Marketing, Brand Strategy, and Psychology. Psychology was definitely my favorite.

» **Middle:** I didn't know much about psychology and I enjoyed learning about all the different aspects of how the mind works.

» **End:** From that class, I now think differently when I am engaged in conversations with people and am very interested in what motivates people.

Right-size the detail—putting it all together

» I have learned that I love understanding what drives people. I had a number of classes that I really enjoyed and three immediately come to mind—Marketing, Brand Strategy, and Psychology. If I choose one, it's definitely psychology. In my past I have taken a lot of math and sciences classes and psychology was all new to me. And I discovered I loved learning about all the different roots of what drives our behavior. Since that class, I'm much more aware of the individual and team dynamics when I'm in a group and thinking about how I can best show up.

Let me dissect that. I started with the headline takeaway that the employer might care about—that I love understanding people (this infers I'm good at interacting with people as well). I used the words "love" and "really enjoyed" to express emotion and passion. These words also communicate positivity. I included a couple other classes to convey a bit more breadth beyond just one. I included an additional message that I am strong in math and science. I got across that I love to learn new things. Finally, I included a little on how I incorporated the learning into how I now operate. All that and it was still concise—probably about a thirty second answer. Not as concise as just answering, "psychology," of course.

Chances are a good interviewer will be curious and dive in more deeply to your stories. In the case of this example, I would want to be prepared to talk about the different roots of human behavior that interested me, as well as some examples of how I showed up more intentional in group settings.

Practice with friends

Storytelling takes practice and your skills will grow over time. You can jumpstart your growth by grabbing a friend who is also serious about their job hunt and practice with each other. I've got some fodder to get you started but please don't be limited by the list. This is not easy. Your stories will not be very compelling the first time through—this all takes practice. Remember, start by thinking about what they are trying to learn about you and the headline that you want to communicate back. Before you start mock interviewing your friend, take some time to think about and discuss what a potential employer might be trying to learn about you with each of these examples:

- » Tell me about a time you found somebody difficult to work with.
- » Tell me about how you go about learning something new.
- » Tell me about a time you took extra initiative.
- » Tell me about a time when you missed a deadline.
- » Tell me about a time you had difficulty communicating with a co-worker.
- » Tell me about the job you had last summer.
- » Tell me about why you picked INSERT major.
- » Tell me about why are interested in working for our company.
- » What is your GPA?
- » What was your favorite class?
- » What was your least favorite class?
- » Why should we hire you?

In an actual interview, always make sure you fully understand the question to ensure you answer the right thing. When we debrief as interviewers, it is not uncommon for me to hear, "They didn't answer the question being asked." That's frustrating and definitely a ding against candidates. If you are unsure, it's okay to ask for clarification. When the interviewer clarifies, their different use of language may make the question click better for you.

Write your answers down

I've got one final recommendation. Once you feel like you have a strong story for a particular question, write it down. Writing it down will reinforce the story flow and help you with recall when you are in an interview situation. I also recommend formulating and writing down your answers for the interview questions you are most scared of being asked. Here are some potentially scary questions:

>   » Why is your GPA low?
>   » Why would we hire you if you have no experience in our industry?
>   » What would you do in your first month on the job?
>   » What's one of your weaknesses and how do you overcome it?
>   » Why do you seem to never stay at the same job very long? (one for later in your career)

Think of some questions that scare you. The more you prepare, the better you will do when under the pressure of an interview for a job you want to land.

Grow your storytelling chops

Practice storytelling. Let's be honest. This is a hard one. You won't wake up tomorrow and be a great storyteller just from reading this. It takes practice. Lots of it. I encourage you to practice with friends. More importantly, I encourage you to attend as many mock or real interviews as you can. That's where your skills will grow the most—when you're under pressure. Keep at it. Remember the building blocks:

- » Consider your audience needs
- » Decide on a compelling headline
- » Build out the story with a start, middle, and end
- » Right-size the detail to bring it to life
- » Tell your story with energy

Don't downplay yourself. Sometimes interview candidates downplay things—a job, their role on a team, a project. If you think and speak as if something is unimportant, you will likely convey that lack of importance to the interviewer. If you think and speak as if something is important, you will likely convey that importance to the interviewer.

Crush the interview—the ultimate test of your social skills

You've worked on a lot of social skills and the interview is the ultimate social interaction to apply all your hard work. By this point, you've already gone through some interviews for on-campus and summer jobs. That's awesome. Think of this section as a handy quick reference to help you crush your full-time role interviews. The list assumes you are going onsite to the company, so skip whatever isn't relevant if you are interviewing on campus.

Before

» Prepare—research the company, the role, and the interviewer(s)

» Identify your three to four questions—the ones that indicate you did a level of research

» Think through the key messages on what you bring, and your relevant illustrative stories

» Print out your résumé so you can show up with hard copies

» Ensure your outfit is ready—shirt/blouse is pressed, and shoes are polished

» Plan your departure time—if driving, know where you will park

Day of—pre-interview

» Groom—shower, brush teeth, groom hair, and clean glasses

» Put on your confidence-boosting outfit—you look sharp

» Leave with plenty of time to arrive early

» Take a moment to breathe and get centered

» Put your phone in airplane mode

» Get in the headspace that this is *the* job you want, not just *a* job you want

» Tell yourself "you got this"—at this point you've done all you can, so be confident

» Greet the receptionist with energy and a smile

» Sit and wait with good posture

Day of—interview

» Greet your interviewer with a strong handshake (if applicable), eye contact, and a smile

» Be conscious of your posture and lean a little forward with eagerness

» Be curious and enthusiastic—really show that you've thought about being in the role

» Illustrate your points with stories

» Read the interviewers non-verbal signals and adjust your detail accordingly

» Close strong and succinctly express that you are excited about the role, have relevant skills, and will look forward to hearing back

Day of—post-interview

» Compose and send a thank you email that reinforces your excitement about the role— remember to be concise, clear, passionate, appreciative, and professional

» Wait to hear back (ugh, the hard part)

In cases where you don't get an offer, ask for feedback so you can learn and improve for next time. There are a variety of company responses to feedback requests. Some may ignore your request, some may give vague feedback that's not actionable, and others may give you specific input that's helpful. Regardless, it's always worth asking. One of my colleagues is in the "business of rejection" in that she is the first person in the organization who says "yes" or "no" to the candidate. Her advice is to begin with a "thank you" and ask succinctly, "Do you have guidance for me that could get me a 'yes' with someone else?" She assures me that request gets a thoughtful, specific answer.

Crush

Prepare. Show up early and get centered. Be present and fully engaged. While the interview reminder list seems long, much of this will become second nature after doing it a few times. As you progress on your search, don't get discouraged. It sometimes takes time for the stars to align and match you up to the right role at the right company. Just keep learning and growing from each interview experience.

Career: Landing the job!

Let's end strong. This is the final leg so don't slow down. Let's start this final career section with another moment of introspection. Then we'll put some final polish on your résumé and dig into actionable recommendations on finding your job. Finally, on a very exciting note, I'll give you some negotiation tips for when you get a verbal offer—something that you definitely will get.

> **Put it all together—embrace your strengths and keep building your muscles**

Ready for some more introspection? This time, I want you to grab a piece of paper and rank the following in order from where you are strongest and feel like you nailed it to where you are weakest and need some work. Some of the items are related to social skills but I've also thrown in career foundation elements as well. Let's look at it all.

Pulse check
» Handshake
» Eye contact
» Speaking volume
» Interviewing attire
» Filler words
» Conversation preparation
» Conversation curiosity and enthusiasm
» Punctuality
» Professional email communications
» Storytelling
» Résumé
» Digital presence—front door
» Digital network building

What's at the top of your list? Embrace those things. Own them. Embrace yourself. Often times, we focus on the things at the bottom of the list and how to improve them. That's important and we'll get there. First though, acknowledge and own your strengths. Keep growing your strengths. Those things where you show up strong might be your secret weapon of differentiation. Wallow.

Did you wallow? Did you really? Do it. Appreciating and extracting confidence from your strengths is important.

Now let's flip the coin. What's at the bottom? You're a senior in college. I don't think I need to lay out much detail on what you need to do about the things at the bottom. Revisit those sections in the book. Make a plan. Commit to the plan. Execute the plan. Boom. Done.

Wallow (in a good way) and keep growing

Take an inventory of your strengths and weaknesses—force rank them. Take time to appreciate your strengths. Own them. Walk in confidence because of them. Think about how to make the most of them when networking and interviewing.

On the other end, what's your plan to keep growing?

Update your résumé, again (and LinkedIn, Handshake, and others)—raise your bar

If you've been following along, your résumé should be current and in a snappy-looking template. Since life is about to get very real, let's give it a final scrub this time. Make sure it includes all your college jobs—both the ones during the school year and those during the summer. How do the bullets look? Are they parallel and consistent? Do they include impact (where relevant) and responsibilities?

Make sure it includes all your compelling college activities, awards, skills, and leadership. Don't forget anything. If your GPA is over 3.5, I would include it. Below that, it may not be a selling point.

At this point, I would strip out all your high school content with one caveat. Keep any exceptional things that you may have achieved like starting a business, going to the Olympics, being high school valedictorian, and other things that support the story thread that you have always taken initiative and achieved results. If you don't have any of those things, no worries.

Get with three to four friends and critique your résumés

Here is where it gets fun, and your résumé will get tight. Ask three or four friends to get together in a room at the library to help each other improve your résumés. Show up with print outs. Focus on one person at a time and go person by person gathering input on what could be improved. Discuss it. Listen and consider differing opinions. I would encourage you to pick friends who are serious about their job search so that the feedback you get is more critical and helpful in finding areas to improve.

Make the edits. Proofread. Have someone else proofread. Save it as a PDF. And now you have your new base résumé. Don't forget to customize it for specific jobs as you apply—mainly the target title and any enhancements you can make in the professional summary section.

Don't forget to make all the same edits on your LinkedIn, Handshake, and other job site and networking profiles too. Proofread. Have someone else proofread.

Raise your résumé bar

Update, critique, and put on your résumé's final polish. Make sure you're showing up consistently across your résumé, LinkedIn, Handshake, and others. Proofread.

> **Go hard at everything your career center offers—panels, mock interviews, and real ones**

Very early in the fall of your senior year is the time to go the Career Center, meet with your friend you made or a new one, and get crystal clear on what is happening when. You do not want to miss out because you didn't know about something. Most likely there will be career panels, mock interview opportunities, and a slew of companies coming on-site to interview and ultimately extend offers. Take advantage of all those things. Think of the Career Center and your job search like an extra class. Let me emphasize, your job hunt starts in the fall, not in the spring.

Career panels can provide ideas, inspiration, and contacts

Here's the deal. Go and sit in the audience and learn. You may get a nugget of wisdom to apply generally to your job search or related to a specific company. I loved something I heard a recruiter tell a room full of students recently. She said, "If you are interviewing with me, I want to feel that this is *the* job you want, not just *a* job you want." I think that is fantastic advice. Use it. Go to other career panels though as there are undoubtedly more gems like that to learn something new or reinforce an idea. Pro tip #1 groom. Pro tip #2 sit near the front. Pro tip #3 don't lay your head on the desk and/or sleep during the panel. This happened recently, and the sleeper was right in the front row. Finally, don't forget to go up and engage with those on the panel who you enjoyed or who work at a company you are targeting.

Mock interviews put you under pressure to be polished and confident

Engage in the mock interviews. Practice. Mock interviews are a great way to up your game on all the things we have covered so far—handshake, eye contact, volume, filler words, punctuality, storytelling, and more. We haven't talked yet about how fast to talk. You want to talk fast enough to show energy, but not so fast that you appear nervous. Talking a little slower also gives you more time to think about your answers.

Ask for honest feedback! When you get constructive feedback, say, "Tell me more." Then ask, "What else could be better?" Keep refining.

On-campus interviews are by far the lightest lift to try and land a job

I will tell you now, signing up for on-campus interviews, interviewing, and potentially getting an offer is by far the lightest lift to landing a job. Take advantage. Those companies are there looking for graduating students from your school—they are looking for you. It couldn't be more targeted. Put significant effort into getting the opportunity to interview on-campus. If you get a job, you'll be happy because you have a job. If you don't get a job, you'll be happy because your skills have grown tremendously from going through the experience.

Embrace everything about the Career Center

Fall in love with your Career Center and everything that it offers. Go to career panels. Go to etiquette dinners. Go to mock interviews. Go to real interviews. If they offer it, you go.

Search for a job like it is your job—dedicate time and commit

If you don't get a job from the fall on-campus interviews, what do you do? First, don't be discouraged. Plenty of students don't land jobs from on-campus recruiting. I didn't, and I turned out okay. You just continue to apply the skills you have already been developing.

Treat job hunting like a job. It's a job that requires a lot of waiting on other people, so isn't something you can do for eight to ten hours a day. That said, I encourage you to dedicate consistent time to it every day. You'll have plenty to do:

» Searching for open roles
» Applying for roles
» Interviewing
» Networking
» Following up

If you dedicate the time, you will get a job. If by chance your new job isn't the killer one that you were hoping for, don't fret. Remember, life is a journey and this is just the start of yours.

Rev up your dedication and perseverance

Dedicate time and persevere. It may not be fun. Nobody said it was. Stay positive. Just know that sometime in the unforeseen future, you will be able to sit across from friends and toast your new job and breathe a deep sigh of relief that your job search is over.

Appreciatively negotiate your offer—don't push too hard

Here we are—my final piece of advice for your senior year. We're going to talk about whether you negotiate your offer or not. My answer is to try, but I personally think you need to tread lightly. I witnessed a friend of mine in graduate school play hardball in his negotiation. While he did end up taking the position, he started with a bit of a stain on his reputation. You don't want that.

Before we talk about how to handle negotiation, I want to highlight the impact a higher offer can have over time. Let's assume you were given an offer of $50k and that you go on to receive a 10% annual raise for the next five years. That salary progression looks like this.

Original offer

Year 1:	$50k
Year 2:	$55k
Year 3:	$61k
Year 4:	$67k
Year 5:	$73k

Now, for easy math, let's pretend you were able to negotiate $60k. That progression looks like this.

Successfully negotiated offer

Year 1:	$60k
Year 2:	$66k
Year 3:	$73k
Year 4:	$80k
Year 5:	$88k

Under the second scenario, five years from now you are making $15k more a year. Across the five years, you would have earned a total of $61k more. That's why it is worth attempting to lightly negotiate. If you do it right, it can't hurt.

Negotiate with the right tenor and exude appreciation

I encourage the following steps to try to get an offer bump, while at the same time being able to start your new position strong and in a positive light.

1. **Express appreciation and excitement.** Express sincere excitement and appreciation when you receive your offer. Thank whoever delivers the news to you. Most likely you will be given the details of your offer verbally and then receive them in writing.

2. **Conduct research to identify any data points you can use as rationale for an increase.** While you are waiting for the written offer, do some research on the compensation for the role. Armed with the job title, you can gather quite a bit of intelligence from online resources like:

   » Glassdoor
   » PayScale
   » Indeed
   » US Bureau of Labor Statistics
   » Other online searches

Temper what you find with your specific geography. You should also reach out to your network to see what you can find out. Based on all that, and any unique and valuable skills you bring, determine the salary number you want, then increase it by $5k. Why not? With a little back and forth, you might land on the number you want.

3. **Again, express appreciation, then tactfully ask.** Asking is not something you will do over email. This needs to be a conversation. Start by again expressing your excitement about the role and then move into the negotiation. Here's my shot at it.

> *Thank you again for the offer. I'm so excited about both the role and COMPANY and I believe I will be a perfect fit to bring value to the team—I have great experience in INSERT and INSERT. I've done some research related to the compensation. Based on that research, and what I bring, would it be possible to increase the base salary to $Xk?*

"Would it be possible" is a very intentional choice of words as it is not demanding in any way. From there, you then bob and weave and play the negotiation game. Just don't push too hard to the point where you come off as appearing difficult. If they can't move on the salary, you could also ask if there is any possibility for a sign-on bonus. Do everything with a positive and eager tone.

   4. Again, express appreciation and excitement.
      Wherever you land, express appreciation for the increase they offer you, or their consideration of your ask. Close reinforcing your excitement about your upcoming start date.

In full transparency, I'm not the best negotiator. I don't like it. If you feel my advice is too soft, there are a couple of popular books on the subject: *Never Split the Difference*, by Chris Voss and *Getting to Yes*, by Roger Fisher and William Ury. Check them out. My preference is to step lightly on that initial negotiation, and then just crush it in terms of job performance to earn raises and promotions.

Negotiate with an appreciative touch

Negotiate while you ensure your appreciation and excitement is front and center. If you do your research, present your request in an appreciative and humble way, if they have money to give, it is likely they will move from the original offer. Good luck!

Senior recap

Early on I congratulated you for being at college. Look where you are now? Congratulations again! Time flies. Make the most of your senior year! Make the most of your job search!

Heart: Getting reflective

» Got clear on some focused actions to make the absolute most out of my Senior year.

Social: Becoming a storyteller

» Learned how to tell a story considering the right amount of detail.
» Gained confidence in my ability to show up solid and confident to interviews.

Career: Landing the job!

» Appreciated my strengths and identified the area(s) I should continue working on.
» Put the final polish on my resume, LinkedIn, Handshake, and other digital presence.
» Attacked everything the Career Center had to offer.
» Dedicated consistent time and energy to my job search.
» Negotiated my offer in an appreciative and excited manner.

Please tell a friend or two how *A Well-Baked Pie* helped you! Kidding, not kidding.

FINAL THOUGHTS

An endorsement for curiosity, positivity, and gumption

If you're still reading, I hope by now you think of me as a trusted advisor. In that role, I have some parting words. There are a bunch of traits and behaviors that enable you to fully show up to your life and career—everyday. Honesty is a foundational one. Pride in your work is another. There are those about showing up as a good human—kindness, caring, love. I like all those. Let's focus and expound on three that I especially endorse and feel strongly about.

Jump out of bed with curiosity

Have a learner-mindset. Why? It's fun. Why not? Why not go through life learning, digging in, growing?

As I mentioned, I've essentially had four different careers along my path, not including learning to be a professor and author. Recently, I went to Toastmasters for a few years as I was curious how to become a more polished speaker—since then I've been an emcee at a number of big work events. When my daughter took piano lessons, I took them too. I read Brené Brown books and listen to Oprah's Super Soul Sunday podcast to expand my emotional and spiritual understanding. I switch gyms periodically to get exposed to new exercises—recently I switched from Orange Theory to a gym that has battle ropes, boxing, hot yoga, and a bunch of classes where I felt like a clown the first time or two. I don't judge on where I start, but where I finish.

See what I did there? I brought my learner-mindset headline to life with a story and some examples. Be curious. It's fun. If you have a learner-mindset you can be open to trying new things and not be scared of failure. You're learning. By the way, let's be real. In addition to all my industrious learning efforts, I also love to vegetate, and I watch a ton of Netflix and Amazon Prime.

Wallow in positivity

Things happen the way they are supposed to happen. They happen for a reason. I believe this. Sometimes it's easy to believe, sometimes it isn't. Not too long ago a position came up at Slalom that I thought should be my next career move. I was very apprehensive to leave my current group and move to the new group but, given my background, skills, and the needs of the organization, I thought that was the path that I should pursue—even perhaps where all the years had been leading. I wanted to fix a mess of a situation and had a clear plan on how to do it. I went for the job. The conversations took about three months. Three months of thinking about what I would do. Turns out, I didn't get it. I was disappointed and, honestly, angry—and that's not really something I get very often. It took the shine off a company I have loved more than any other. I kept telling myself that things happen the way they are supposed to happen. I said it over and over—I wasn't feeling it though. I felt guilty for not trusting my belief that things happen for a reason. I knew my belief was being tested.

Things happen the way they are supposed to happen. Just a couple months later there was a shuffle in my current group. I got two new teams in addition to the one I've enjoyed working with for the last couple of years. There are some amazing people on all my teams and I'm reinvigorated by the new challenges—I love showing up every day. I don't think that would have been true for the role I was pursuing. But here is the big deal: if I had taken that other role, I would have been fully diving in and fixing things. I highly doubt I would have woken up one day over my holiday break and decided to write a book. So, things really do happen the way they are supposed to happen. Test given. Test taken. Test passed.

Believing that things happen for a reason is a foundation for positivity. When things go wrong, ask what you should be learning from the situation. Sure, you can get sad, mad, and/or disappointed but let it pass. Don't dwell. Know that there is a reason. You just can't always see the reason at the time.

Beyond that, exude enthusiasm. Be grateful for what you have, not lamenting what you don't.

Show up with gumption

I love grit. I struggled whether I wanted to leave you with grit or gumption. By mentioning grit, I'm leaving you with both. Have grit.

Let's talk about gumption though. The definition includes resourcefulness, courage, common sense, shrewdness. Related words include savvy, cleverness, spirit, and my favorite, get-up-and-go. Giddy up. Can you envision showing up to life with gumption? To your job search? To your new job? Gumption will get you far. Plus, it is fun to say. Gumption.

That's all. Bye for now. Get out there and launch into your career.

Your final recap! bring it home

Oh, here is one final recap for you. Enjoy the fact that you made it through this book. More importantly, enjoy your new job!

» Worked on my seven essential ingredients to become an irresistible pie

» Finished this weirdo book about all kinds of pie.

» Got a job to start what is going to be my amazing career journey.

ACKNOWLEDGMENTS

I have a lot of people to thank for helping me with this book!

First, thank you to my family! My peeps Tracy, Bennet, and Greta who always support me. My mom and dad who instilled me with drive and are always there with a guiding word. My step-mom Janet whose been a friend for 20+ years now. You are all very special to me and there aren't words to thank you for how you have shaped me and supported me on life's journey.

Next up, my Slalom colleagues and their families! First, Andrew Houston for the initial inspiration to write a book. Mark Tindall and his wife Sally Bjornsen who educated me on how book agents and publishers work. Our recruiters Kim Bourget and Jessi Stephen (who I am forever grateful to for recruiting me to Slalom) who helped me hone the content. Mike Walters and his wife Deb who help provide the high school counselor perspective. Tessa King and her mom Nancy for providing that power student and power mom lens. Steve Muran and his son Cole for the timely take on what his helpful. And Maggie Hamilton, Josh McGrew, Sabina Nawaz, Laura Parker, Alikhan Pirmohamed, Rachel Olmsted, and Jen Travis for taking the time to provide input and ideas. Thank you all.

My friends at Seattle University were a huge help too. Thank you to Megan Spaulding and Mary Lou Moffat for providing your thoughts from a career center and student coaching perspective. Also, thanks to those I had the pleasure of being in a mentor/mentee relationship with including Cameron Clark, Kelsey Hofmann, Jessica Notman, and Nianzu Yan.

Finally, thank you so much to Maryann Karinch for taking a chance on me. Trying to land a publisher during a worldwide pandemic that started with the shutdown of New York was not an easy ask. I so appreciate you continuing to believe that this content would be helpful to get out into the world.

Much love and gratitude to you all.

b.

About the Author

Brian Ladyman is a Managing Director at Slalom Consulting and an Adjunct Professor at Albers School of Business and Economics at Seattle University— where he teaches Strategic Brand Management. He has an MBA from Dartmouth, and a BS from Pepperdine University. His leadership career has been an immersive learning journey across a plethora of industries and roles—with heavy emphasis in the technology sector and marketing functions. While the Pacific Northwest is his base, he has also called the Northeast, Southeast, Midwest, and West all home, as well as London and Sydney. He currently lives in a suburb of Seattle with his wife, Tracy, and their Cocker Spaniel, Oscar.